CHOICES

WRITING PROJECTS
FOR
STUDENTS OF ESL

Carole Turkenik
American Language Institute
New York University

CAMBRIDGE
UNIVERSITY PRESS

PUBLISHED BY THE PRESS SYNDICATE OF THE UNIVERSITY OF CAMBRIDGE
The Pitt Building, Trumpington Street, Cambridge, United Kingdom

CAMBRIDGE UNIVERSITY PRESS
The Edinburgh Building, Cambridge CB2 2RU, UK   http://www.cup.cam.ac.uk
40 West 20th Street, New York, NY 10011–4211, USA   http://www.cup.org
10 Stamford Road, Oakleigh, Melbourne 3166, Australia
Ruiz de Alarcón 13, 28014 Madrid, Spain

First published by St. Martin's Press, Inc.

Reprinted 1999

Printed in the United States of America

Library of Congress Cataloging-in-Publication Data Available

ISBN 0 521 65793 8 Student's Book
ISBN 0 521 65794 6 Instructor's Manual

PREFACE

There are many understandings of what constitutes "good" writing and many routes to its achievement. *Choices* leads students on a journey of exploration into what the English-speaking academic community considers good writing and encourages students to discover their own pathway to its achievement.

The book is intended for low-intermediate to intermediate-level students. It is aimed particularly at students who wish to pursue academic studies in English-speaking institutions, but it could also be used profitably in intensive, general English courses for teens or adults. It is designed for a thirteen-to-fifteen week course.

Choices utilizes a process approach to writing. It gives students the opportunity to first think, talk, and read about a topic. Then it divides the task of writing into stages, gives students a chance to practice each of the steps, and introduces a variety of approaches to these different steps.

Overall, the book strives to encourage students to find their own writing style, to provide them with strategies they can use in future writing assignments, and to give them a feeling of independence and control over the improvement of their own writing.

UNDERLYING ASSUMPTIONS

The book rests on five interrelated assumptions. The first is that there is no one way to write and no single series of steps that all writers follow. Each writer must discover what works best for him or her. However, while students are learning a new language and culture, they can be receptive to learning new ways to write. Hence the text introduces a variety of approaches for students to try.

The second assumption is that the acquisition of writing competence does not follow a linear progression from sentence to paragraph to essay. Hence the text follows a "top down" approach that begins immediately with essay writing and examines paragraphs and sentences as integral elements of essays rather than a "bottom up" approach that asks students to master sentences and paragraphs first before progressing to essays.

The third assumption is that the users of this book are educated adults (young and not so young) who enter our classes with knowledge and experience, including at least some experience of writing in their native language. Hence they can benefit from discussions about writing and about the expectations of native English speakers, and how these expectations may differ from those of their own language.

The fourth assumption is that although discussing rules and techniques is valuable, students ultimately learn to write by struggling to write. Thus the book offers few writing exercises but many opportunities for writing and rewriting.

The last assumption is that writing and grammar are related but different phenomena. Grammar provides the underpinning for writing (as it does for all of language), but good writing and grammatical accuracy are not synonymous. Hence, the book separates writing and grammar, and focusses primarily on the development and organization of ideas and secondarily on the correction of form.

ORGANIZATION

The book is divided into two sections. The first part, which forms the major portion of the text, deals with writing. The second part deals with grammar.

The first part consists of five chapters, each focussed on a different topic. All the activities in the chapter revolve around the topic; hence each chapter is referred to as a project. The project titles are: The Real Me, Thinking about Writing, New Lives, Teachers and Learners, and Choosing a Career. In each project, students are introduced to the topic through discussion and reading, guided through the process of writing a complete essay (prewriting, drafting, revising, and editing), and given more intensive practice in a particular writing skill or aspect of essay organization. At-home essay assignments and corollary journal writing provide students with additional writing opportunities and the chance to try other forms of writing.

The second part of the book contains explanations of a number of grammar points—chosen for their importance to writing clarity and their accessibility to student correction—and gives students practice in correcting errors in these areas. Students then apply this knowledge to editing their own writing. The grammar points covered include basic sentence components (subject-verb-object or complement), verb tense and form, subject-verb and noun-quantifier agreement, sentence boundaries, pronoun use, and punctuation.

GUIDELINES FOR USE

The text treats writing and editing as cumulative skills; hence, the projects are best tackled in the order given. Within each project, however, the materials are not intended to be used strictly in the order of presentation. Each project presents first all the steps of the writing process followed by discussion and practice of writing skills; the related grammar section appears at the end of the text. These three sections are intended to be interwoven. The pointing finger icon tells students when to move ahead to the appropriate section. The shifts are also discussed in the *Instructor's Manual*.

SPECIAL FEATURES

- **The text utilizes themes as an organizational framework and integrates all the discussion, reading, writing, and grammar in each chapter within the context of the theme.** This thematic approach allows students to explore a topic from many different perspectives and to write about it in a variety of ways. It also allows practice of specific rhetorical forms to follow from the nature of the assignment rather than as an end in itself.

- **The text stresses the value of collaboration and outside input at certain stages in the writing process.** Each project includes group discussion prior to writing as a way of generating ideas about a subject, pair or group response during the composing stage to get a reader's reaction to a draft prior to revision, and pair work again at the editing stage to provide an additional check on the grammatical accuracy of the writing.

- **The text facilitates peer response through a series of specific guide questions.** These questions, which appear on the Reader Response Sheets, direct students in what to look for when responding to their classmates' essays. The guide questions change with each assignment to reflect the particular focus of the project.

- **The text uses authentic passages by experienced writers as readings and writing samples.** The passages vary in content, style, and authorship. Contributors include men and women, teenagers and adults, native and non-native speakers, and professional and nonprofessional writers. However, because the readings also serve to illustrate how English writers deal with common writing problems, only passages written originally in English have been included.

- **The text uses authentic student writing to illustrate writing problems and revision techniques and provide practice in grammar correction.** These examples illustrate the kinds of essays intermediate-level students produce, the types of writing and grammar problems they encounter, and the ways they deal with them.

- **The text emphasizes students' own experiences as a source of ideas to write about and at the same time teaches writing skills necessary for academic success.** The essay assignments ask students to draw on their own knowledge and experience rather than on information learned from assigned readings. This focus on personal experience gives all students access to ideas to write about regardless of academic interests or background knowledge and also engages students more actively, thus enabling them to have a more satisfying writing experience. At the same time, however, the text teaches academic writing in that students are asked to analyze this personal data in ways similar to those required in content courses (defining, comparing, generalizing, etc.).

- **The text emphasizes essay writing but also provides students with opportunities to practice other kinds of academic writing tasks.** In addition to writing essays, students take notes, answer questions, and write explanations and suggestions.

- **The text includes journal writing that is thematically related to the writing projects.** Each chapter provides a list of prompts for journal writing. The prompts always relate to the project theme, but they vary in nature (including sayings, quotations, reading passages, and cartoons) and give students the chance to explore a topic in many different ways.

- **The text stresses the importance of accuracy in writing but reserves grammar for the editing stage of the writing process.** By attending to writing first and grammar second, but then focussing explicitly on correction in the editing phase, the text emphasizes the importance of grammar as an element of—though not a substitute for—good writing. Given the assurance that attention to form is not being ignored, but merely delayed, students can be less fearful and less inhibited writers.

- **The text views all the writing that a student produces during the semester as a corpus of material that the writer can continue to work on.** It asks students to keep all their writing and to go back to their earlier efforts as sources of material for revision. This enables students to see improvement in their writing and encourages them to view writing as an ongoing process. It also permits end-of-term assessment by either portfolio or examination.

The *Instructor's Manual* that accompanies this text includes a discussion of the aims and audience for *Choices*; a description of the organization of the text; an outline of the contents; and suggestions for using the text as a whole as well as the individual projects, additional writing assignments, journal writing topics, and additional readings. Also included are a suggested course plan (for a 13–15 week semester) and answers to exercises in the text.

A FINAL NOTE

My interest in developing these materials was stimulated by the process writing texts for advanced ESL students (especially those by Ann Raimes, Nancy Arapoff Cramer, and Trudy Smoke) that began to appear in the mid-1980s. These books pioneered the notion that advanced-level students, although not fully skilled in English, could profit from learning and engaging in the writing process used by successful writers. I felt that my intermediate students were no different; they were just less proficient in English and less familiar with the characteristics of the English writing style. I wanted them to have the same advantage as their more advanced peers, the same opportunity to improve their writing by learning about and engaging actively in the process of writing.

I believe my students have benefitted from this approach; I know they have had fun. I hope yours do too.

ACKNOWLEDGMENTS

So many people contributed threads of ideas to this book that I could never sort out all the strands. However a number of people gave heroically of their thoughts and time and deserve special note.

Thanks to my students, first at Queens College of the City University of New York and later at New York University, whose struggles to learn to write in English inspired me to develop the materials that led to this book and whose experiences helped to give it its final shape; to Claire Howard, a friend and colleague at Queens College, who tested the materials over many semesters and provided invaluable feedback from her experiences; and to Kathleen O'Reilly at New York University, who also offered ideas and encouragement.

Thanks, too, to Naomi Silverman, my editor at St. Martin's Press, who rescued the project, shared her love of cartoons, and showed unwavering enthusiasm and conviction; and to the editorial staff at St. Martin's, especially Carl Whithaus and my project editor Amy Horowitz, who displayed great patience in answering my questions and dealing with the minutiae of getting this book into print.

Thanks to my reviewers whose thoughtful comments and helpful suggestions did much to make this a better book: Maureen Burke, University of Iowa; Denis Hall, New Hampshire College; Martha Low, University of Oregon, Eugene; Michael Masyn, University of Colorado, Boulder; Joanna McKenzie, California State University, Northridge; Heidimarie H. Rambo, Kent State University; Mary Ellen Ryder, Boise State University; and Nancy Strickland, El Paso Community College.

Finally, special thanks to my husband and children who provided unquestioning support and who put up with the hundreds of days and nights when I abandoned them for my computer and left them with the dishes and the laundry.

Carole Turkenik

CONTENTS

GRAMMAR   179

INTRODUCTION: TO THE STUDENT

As you begin this course, you will probably have many questions. Perhaps you can find some of the answers here.

What is this book about?

First and foremost, this book is about *writing*. It is not a grammar book. Many students who are still struggling to learn the structure of English, as you are, think that if only they could write "correctly," all their writing problems would be solved. But writing is not just a matter of constructing grammatically correct sentences and using correct spelling and punctuation. Grammar, spelling, and punctuation are important, of course, and you will work to improve them. But *real writing* is about ideas and clearly communicating those ideas to other people. That is the focus of this book.

Second, this book is about the *process of writing*. The dictionary defines *process* as "a connected series of actions or steps leading to a certain result." The process of writing, then, is the set of actions or steps that all writers go through in transferring ideas from mind to paper. The particular steps may vary from writer to writer, but every writer must deal with the process.

Last of all, this book is about *becoming a more independent writer*. Now you have a teacher and classmates to help you improve your writing. But in examinations and out-of-class assignments and when your English courses end, you will have to rely on your own ability to improve your writing. So you will work on learning how you can make your own writing better.

What kind of writing will I do?

In class you will focus on essay writing. An essay is a form of writing that attempts to inform the reader about something, explain a position or problem, or persuade someone about something. It is one of the main types of writing students must do in university courses.

I wrote essays in my own country. Why do I have to learn how to write them again?

To write successfully in English, you cannot just use the composition forms that you learned in your native country. American English, like all languages, has its own rules of how opinions should be expressed, how ideas should be developed, and how information should be organized. These probably differ from the style rules you learned in your native country. So you will examine the form of an American English essay and practice writing in this style.

What will I write about?

Most of the time you will write about your own thoughts and opinions. You will use your own experiences as a source of ideas. Many of you have never been asked to write about your own lives and thoughts, but in fact all of you have a wealth of experiences that can serve as a basis for your essays.

Is essay writing the only kind of writing I will do?

No. Although essay writing is the primary focus of this class, it is not the only kind of writing you will do. You will also take notes, answer questions, and write letters, dialogues, and descriptions. Most of this other kind of writing you will do in a *journal*.

What is a journal?

A journal is a notebook in which you record your thoughts, feelings, ideas, and opinions. Several times a week you will be given a topic (for example, a saying, a quotation, a cartoon, or a reading passage) to think about and respond to in your journal. All the topics will be related to the subject of the essay you are working on, and some of the ideas you develop in your journal may help you in writing your essay. But primarily your journal is a place where you can explore your thoughts more freely and improve your ability to express yourself in written English.

All journal writing will be done at home. Although your teacher may check to see that you are doing the assignments, they will not be corrected. Instead, every few weeks you will share some of your journal entries with your classmates.

What is the difference between journal writing and essay writing?

Essays follow a specific form. In your journal, you can write in a much looser or less structured way than you could in an essay. You can write whatever comes to your mind about a topic without concern for essay organization.

How much writing will I have to do?

The answer is *a lot*! So be prepared. Writing is like driving a car or playing tennis. You can discuss how to do it, you can read about how to do it, you can listen to a teacher talk about how to do it—and these can be helpful. But in the end the only way to learn and to improve your writing is to write. And to write often. The more you practice, the better you will get.

Thus, over the semester you will work on five writing projects. Each project has a different topic, and each requires at least one essay in addition to your journal writing and other assignments.

Will this course be like other writing classes I have taken?

Maybe not. In past writing classes, you may have written a weekly composition that you gave to your teacher to be corrected and graded. You did all or most of the writing at home and your teacher only saw the composition you handed in. How you arrived at that final version was not important. Here, because we are concerned with the *process* of writing, everything you write is important and part of the record of your writing. Thus, everything you write you will save as a kind of history of the assignment.

Also in the past, your teacher probably corrected all your grammar errors or at least showed you where you had made mistakes. But in this class, you will practice looking for and correcting your own grammar errors.

These answers keep referring to the "process of writing." I am still not sure what that means.

No writer magically produces an essay or an article or a book. No writer sits down and comes up with a perfectly organized and perfectly worded piece of writing on the first try. All writing, no matter what language it is written in, is the result of the writer's effort and struggle to decide what he or she wants to say and how best to say it. What you eventually read is the end result of thinking and writing, and rethinking and rewriting, and more rethinking and more rewriting. This is what we mean by the *process of writing*.

The writing process can be divided into steps. Sometimes this process moves forward directly in a straight line like this:

But more often it moves haphazardly forwards and backwards in overlapping fashion like this:

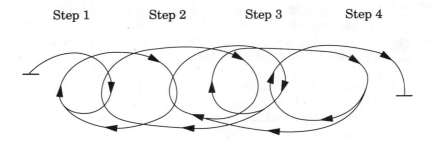

In class, you will look at each of the steps in the writing process from the beginning step of generating ideas to write about, through the intermediate steps of determining what you want to say and how best to say it, to the final step of producing a grammatically correct and polished piece of writing that is ready for evaluation. Each of these steps is equally important in the writing process; together they show how a piece of writing was produced. Thus whenever you write an essay, you will save your work from each step so that when you finish the assignment, you will have a complete record of the process you went through.

Now before you continue reading, take a few moments to think and talk about the writing you do outside of school. Ask yourself the following questions.

1. Do you ever write anything that is not required for a class? If so, what do you write? How often do you write?

2. Have you ever kept a diary or a journal? Why or why not?

3. Is there any difference between a diary and a journal? If so, what do you think the difference is?

The author of the following essay, Joseph Reynolds, is an English teacher in an American high school as well as a writer who has published articles in newspapers and magazines. He is also a long-time journal keeper, so when he talks about the value of journal writing, he is speaking from his own experience. This essay is titled "I Think (and Write in a Journal), Therefore I Am."

° **Samuel Johnson:** 18th-century English writer
° **Descartes:** 17th-century French philosopher
° **dictum:** saying
° **keenly:** intensely, deeply
° **subtle:** hardly noticeable

"I write, therefore I am," wrote Samuel Johnson,° altering Descartes'° famous dictum:° "I think, therefore I am."

When writing in my journal, I feel keenly° alive and somehow get a glimpse of what Johnson meant.

My journal is a storehouse, a treasure for everything in my daily life: the stories I hear, the people I meet, the quotations I like, and even the subtle° signs and symbols I encounter that speak to me indirectly. Unless I capture these things in writing, I lose them.

All writers are such collectors, whether they keep a journal or not; they see life clearly, a vision we only recognize when reading their books. . . .

° **craftsman:** highly skilled worker
° **stoop:** small porch with steps at the door to a house
° **hone:** sharpen
° **prose:** ordinary writing (not poetry)
° **harbor:** hold
° **arena:** enclosed space where sports are played
° **idly:** not working

By writing in my own journal, I often make discoveries. I see connections and conclusions that otherwise would not appear obvious to me. I become a craftsman,° like a potter or a carpenter who makes a vase or a wooden stoop° out of parts. Writing is a source of pleasure when it involves such invention and creation.

I want to work on my writing, too, hone° it into clear, readable prose,° and where better to practice my writing than in my journal. Writing, I'm told, is a skill, and improves with practice. I secretly harbor° this hope. So my journal becomes the arena° where I do battle with the written word.

Sometimes when I have nothing to write, I sit idly° and thumb back through old entries. I rediscover incidents long forgotten.

During a recent cold midwinter night, for example, I reread an entry dated a summer ago. My wife and I had just returned after a day at the beach. We were both tired and uncomfortable after the long ride home, but our spirits were lifted when we saw our cat come down the driveway to greet us, her tail held high shouting her presence. By reading this entry, I relived the incident, warming with affection for my cat and a sunny day at the beach.

I always try to write something, however, even if it is free writing, writing anything that comes to mind. Often this process is a source of a "core° idea" that can later be developed into a more finely polished piece of writing. The articles I've published had their inception° in my journal.

° **core:** most important or central part
° **inception:** beginning

Journal writing, in addition, is a time when I need not worry about the rules of spelling and grammar; it provides a relaxed atmosphere in which my ideas and feelings can flow freely onto the page. If I discover an idea worth developing, then [I rewrite].

My journal becomes a place where I can try different kinds of writing, as well, from prose and poetry to letters to the editor. Attempting different kinds is useful . . . my writing improves.

° **solitude:** the state of being alone, away from other people
° **omniscient:** all-knowing, knowing everything

When I write in my journal, I seek the solitude° of my study. With pen in hand, I become omniscient;° I am aware of the quiet, damp, night air, or the early-morning sounds of life. My journal is the place where I discover life.

. . . for these few moments, at least, . . . I am.

Remove this sheet and tape it to the inside front cover of your journal notebook so you can refer to it easily and quickly.

■ ■

JOURNAL INSTRUCTIONS

1. Start each journal entry on a clean, right-hand page. On the top line, write the assignment number on the left and the date on the right.

2. Below the assignment number and date, in the center of the line, write the title of your entry.

3. Now comes the big question: *What do I write about?* Well, you can write about anything the assignment makes you think about. Don't analyze the assignment; you are writing a journal, not a literature project. Don't write what it says in different words; that's a valuable exercise, but it's not journal writing. Instead, respond to the topic. Write about your own thoughts. What does it make you think about? What ideas does it bring to your mind? What are your thoughts while you read it? What are your thoughts after you read it? Do you agree or disagree with it? Did it make you laugh, or cry, or feel sad, or feel angry? Why? Have you ever had an experience like this? How did you react to it? Write from your heart.

4. You can write as much as you want, but you must write *at least one page* each time, single spaced. If you double space, write two pages. And try to write when you are awake and energetic and have time to sit down and think, not at 2 A.M. when you are about to collapse from exhaustion or at 8:25 A.M. while you are on the bus rushing to class.

PROJECT

1

THE REAL ME

In this project, you will

- think about how to discover ideas to write about.
- practice one way to get those ideas down on paper: listing.
- learn what a paragraph is and what an essay is.
- look at the relationship of ideas in a paragraph and an essay.
- work on several writing assignments that will help your classmates get to know you better.
- begin to practice being a critical reader of writing.
- start to edit your own writing.
- begin writing in your journal.

GETTING IDEAS

*Writing is no trouble; you just jot down ideas as they occur to you.
The jotting is simplicity itself—it is the occurring which is difficult.*

STEPHEN LEACOCK

The first step in the writing process is getting ideas to write about. Many student writers complain that this is their greatest problem. They say that sometimes they can't think of anything to say about a topic. Their minds are blank. There are solutions, however.

Getting Ideas by Brainstorming

One way to get ideas about a subject is to focus your thoughts on it and then let your mind run free in all directions around it. Let your mind release a storm of ideas. This process is called *brainstorming*. To *brainstorm* means to think of as many ideas as you can about a subject in a short period of time.

In most cases your mind is not really empty at all. You really do have lots of ideas from your many years of reading, thinking, and experiencing. If nothing comes out, if your mind seems blank, it is probably because you are so worried that your ideas are wrong or silly or unrelated that you reject your ideas just as soon as you think of them. Don't! In brainstorming, anything goes. All ideas are worth considering. What seems silly at first might turn out later not to be silly at all or it might lead you to another, really good idea. And if the idea turns out to be truly silly, at least you can have a good laugh.

> To brainstorm, relax, let your thoughts flow, and let your mind explore in all directions.

Brainstorming is a good technique to help you come up with ideas that you can develop into an essay. By letting your thoughts run free, you can discover new ideas that you never realized you had; you can open your mind to different ways of looking at a subject; and you can conquer *writer's block*—the feeling that you have nothing to write about.

Some of you probably brainstorm already at least some of the time. So perhaps you are saying, "My problem is not a lack of ideas, but rather I have so many ideas that I feel confused. When I start to write, so many ideas crowd into my mind and compete for my attention that I can't make any sense out of them."

Well, the real problem is not having too many ideas—you can never have too many ideas. The problem is trying to do too many things at one time. You are trying to think of ideas, remember them, evaluate them, organize them, and write a composition all at the same time.

The solution is to separate these steps. Before you start writing your composition, brainstorm and write your ideas down. Even for native speakers of a language it is almost impossible to think of ideas, assess the ideas, and organize the ideas simultaneously. So first concentrate on generating ideas and writing them down. Brainstorming is truly useful only if you get the ideas down on paper before you start your essay.

To brainstorm on paper, write down all your thoughts as fast as you can. Don't worry about grammar or spelling or the order of your ideas. Don't correct what you write. Don't use a dictionary. If you can't think of a word in English, write it in your native language. Later, if you decide to use this idea, you can look the word up. *Your notes are not a composition; they are for your own personal use.* And remember to write down even ideas that may seem silly or unrelated to the topic; you can eliminate whatever is inappropriate later.

There are many different methods of brainstorming. Here you will try one way. In other projects, you will try other methods.

Brainstorming Method 1: Listing

Probably the most common way to write down ideas is to *list* them. *Listing* means writing down each idea on a separate line. You don't need to write complete sentences; words or phrases are fine. And you can write the ideas in whatever order they come to mind. For example, to write an essay on "The Advantages of Brainstorming," I brainstormed for five minutes and came up with the following list:

> helps remember my ideas
> helps untangle ideas
> starts my pen moving
> shakes cobwebs out of my brain
> gets my brain moving
> can organize thoughts
> can see repetition of ideas
> prewriting is funny word.
> brainstorming is funnier word
> makes me think I'm doing something useful
> keeps my mind focussed on writing
> can order ideas
> can choose best examples
> looking at ideas helps judge them
> uses more paper — helps paper companies

At the end of the five minutes, I looked back at my list and thought about my ideas so far. I specifically considered two questions. First, what is the objective or *purpose* of my essay and which of my ideas best fits that purpose? Second, what *audience* am I writing this for; who is going to read my essay and what information do they need? I then eliminated some of my ideas and kept the rest to think about some more and eventually to write about.

Purpose

Whenever we write, we have a purpose in mind. We are trying to do something specific. We may want to

- inform our readers about a subject they don't know much about.
- persuade our readers to agree with our opinion or point of view.

- explain or define some concept or idea.
- entertain our readers by being funny or beautiful or dramatic.

Thinking about our purpose helps us to decide which of our ideas are more appropriate.

Audience

When we write something, we usually intend it to be read by someone else. For students, the audience may be other students in the class either from the same country or from a different country; it may be the class teacher; or it may be other students or teachers who are unknown to the writer. For people who work, the readers may be colleagues, a manager or boss, or clients. In each case, however, our readers have special needs that we must consider. Thinking directly about who our readers—our audience—will be helps us to decide what ideas we need to include.

CLASS EXERCISE

An English class in your native country has asked you to write an article in English about your impressions of this country. Specifically, your readers want to know: *What are the people like?*

Start thinking about this topic and call out whatever ideas come to your mind. Don't censor any of your ideas or stop to think whether your ideas are appropriate or "right." Your teacher will write them all down on the blackboard so you can see them and think about them.

Next look at the list of ideas you generated. Are there any that don't answer the question in the assignment? Cross them out. Think about your purpose and audience. Are there any ideas that don't suit this purpose or this group of readers? Cross them out. Are there any ideas that on second thought you don't agree with or don't really know very much about? Cross them out. Are there any ideas that are very similar? Group them together or draw arrows to connect them.

Now you have discovered what you know about the topic, and you have some ideas you could write about.

Brainstorming Practice

Now you are going to try brainstorming by yourself.

1. Brainstorm for five minutes on the topic " The Qualities That I Admire in a Person" (*Note:* a *quality* is something characteristic of a person. For example, kindness, patience, or honesty). Write whatever comes to your mind, and list your ideas one below the other. Remember, you don't need to write complete sentences. Use the space provided on the next page for your brainstorming.

_____

_____

_____

_____

_____

_____

_____

_____

_____

_____

_____

_____

_____

_____

2.   Now look back at your list and choose one of your ideas: the quality you think is the most interesting, the most important, or the one you know the most about. Circle it and write it here.

Idea: _____

3.   Next brainstorm this one idea further in the space provided below. List all the thoughts that come to your mind about it. For example, explain what you think the word means, or give reasons why you admire the quality, or describe occasions when you or someone else showed this quality.

_____

_____

_____

_____

_____

_____

_____

_____

_____

_____

_____

_____

_____

4.   Finally, on a separate sheet of paper write a paragraph on "The Quality That I Most Admire in a Person." Include some or all of the ideas you came up with in your brainstorming.

More Brainstorming Practice

1.   Brainstorm for five minutes on the topic "Why I Chose This School." In the space below, list all the reasons you can think of.

_____

_____

_____

_____

_____

_____

_____

_____

_____

_____

_____

_____

_____

2.   Look back at your list. Are there any ideas that can be grouped together? Join them with arrows. Are there any ideas that are not directly related to the question? Cross them out. Now think about your purpose and your audience (your readers), and choose two or three different reasons to focus on. You can choose the more important ones, the more interesting ones, or the ones you know most about. Circle these two or three ideas. Check: Are they really different reasons? If not, think and choose again.

3.   In the space below and on the next page, write down each of the reasons you have chosen. Then brainstorm each reason. Explain it, give more information about it, or give an example of it. Write in list form.

Reason 1: _____

_____

_____

_____

_____

_____

_____

_____

_____

Reason 2: _____

_____

_____

_____

_____

_____

_____

_____

Reason 3: _____

_____

_____

_____

_____

_____

_____

_____

_____

_____

4. Write an essay titled "Why I Chose This School" using some or all of the ideas you have come up with.

STARTING TO THINK ABOUT THE TOPIC OF THIS PROJECT

You have practiced listing as a way to brainstorm on paper. Now you can try listing to help you get some ideas about the topic of this project.

For this first project, you are going to think about yourself. Each of you is unique. Each of you is different from everyone else. Each of you has your own personality, your own set of characteristics or qualities.

Brainstorm for five minutes on "The Qualities that Make Me Unique." List at least ten adjectives or phrases that describe you. They can be positive or negative. Use the space on the next page for your brainstorming list.

_____

_____

_____

_____

_____

_____

_____

_____

_____

_____

_____

_____

_____

_____

Getting Ideas through Reading

1. Have you ever felt that you were ugly? Why?

2. What makes someone handsome or beautiful? What makes someone ugly?

3. Have you ever been dissatisfied with some aspect of your appearance, for example, your height or weight, your hair, your nose or teeth or legs, or your skin color?

Richard Rodriguez is a well-known Mexican-American author who wrote about his passage from childhood to adulthood in an autobiography titled _Hunger of Memory_. In the excerpt below, he describes the feelings he had as a child about his skin color.

° **complexion:** skin color and appearance, especially on the face
° **feo:** Spanish for ugly

° **swirling:** moving round and round

° **fashioned:** made
° **lather:** soap suds

° **flesh:** skin

° **adolescence:** young teenage years

[I felt ashamed] because of my dark complexion.° I was . . . an ugly child. Or one who thought himself ugly. (_Feo._°) One night when I was eleven or twelve years old, I locked myself in the bathroom and carefully regarded my reflection in the mirror over the sink. Without any pleasure I studied my skin. I turned on the faucet. (In my mind I heard the swirling° voices of aunts, and even my mother's voice, whispering. . . about lemon juice solutions and dark, _feo_ children.) With a bar of soap, I fashioned° a thick ball of lather.° I began soaping my arms. I took my father's straight razor out of the medicine cabinet. Slowly, with steady deliberateness, I put the blade against my flesh,° pressed it as close as I could without cutting, and moved it up and down across my skin to see if I could get out, somehow lessen, the dark. All I succeeded in doing, however, was in shaving my arms bare of their hair. For as I noted with disappointment, the dark would not come out. It remained. Trapped. Deep in the cells of my skin.

Throughout adolescence,° I felt myself mysteriously marked. Nothing else about my appearance would concern me so much as the fact that my

° **braces:** wires worn on the teeth to straighten them
° **profile:** side view

complexion was dark. My mother would say how sorry she was that there was not money enough to get braces° to straighten my teeth. But I never bothered about my teeth. In three-way mirrors at department stores, I'd see my profile° dramatically defined by a long nose, but it was really only the color of my skin that caught my attention.

° **menial laborer:** person who works at a low paying, physically difficult job
° **vulnerable:** easily hurt, sensitive
° **abuse:** mistreatment, attack

I wasn't afraid that I would become a menial laborer° because of my skin. Nor did my complexion make me feel especially vulnerable° to racial abuse.° (I didn't really consider my dark skin to be a racial characteristic. I would have been only too happy to look as Mexican as my light-skinned older brother.) Simply, I judged myself ugly. And, since the women in my family had been the ones who discussed it in such worried tones, I felt my dark skin made me unattractive to women.

° **grammar school:** elementary school

° **tone:** color

Thirteen years old. Fourteen. In a grammar school° art class, when the assignment was to draw a self-portrait, I tried and I tried but could not bring myself to shade in the face on the paper to anything like my actual tone.° With disgust then I would come face to face with myself in mirrors. With disappointment I located myself in class photographs—my dark face undefined by the camera which had clearly described the white faces of classmates. Or I'd see my dark wrist against my long-sleeved white shirt.

° **listless:** lacking energy or desire to move

I grew divorced from my body. Insecure, overweight, listless.°

Getting More Ideas through Discussion

Another way of getting ideas about a topic is to talk to other people. Through discussion and the sharing of your thoughts, you can generate more ideas than if you just work alone. So the next step in this project is to talk about the topic with your classmates.

As a group, answer the discussion questions below. Everyone must participate and share ideas. If you cannot understand what someone says, ask for an explanation. Write down all your group members' ideas in the space provided. Taking notes like this is another form of writing that you will need for classes, seminars, and meetings.

Discussion Questions

1. What do you think are your best qualities? What do you think are your worst qualities? For the first table, ask each member of the group to name his or her most negative characteristics and to describe how they are shown in his or her behavior. The first space is filled in as an example.

NAME	WORST QUALITIES	DESCRIPTION
James	impatient	I don't let people finish what they're saying. I always interrupt.
	very critical	I'm too quick to find fault in others.
1.		

2.		
3.		
4.		

Now ask each member of the group to name his or her most positive characteristics and to describe how they are shown in his or her behavior.

NAME	BEST QUALITIES	DESCRIPTION
1.		
2.		
3.		
4.		

2.   Do you think a person can change his or her personality? If so, how? If not, why not? Discuss this question as a group. Then in the space below, write a summary of your group's ideas.

_____

_____

_____

_____

_____

_____

_____

_____

_____

_____

_____

_____

ESSAY TOPICS FOR PROJECT 1

By now you should have a lot of ideas about the topic of this project, so it is time to start writing an essay. Choose one of the following assignments.

1.   No one is perfect, but everyone has some positive characteristics, some good qualities, that he or she feels proud of. What do you think are the best aspects of your character?

2.   Many people are not satisfied with themselves as they are. They look at themselves and see habits or qualities they don't like. What aspects of your character would you like to change?

PREWRITING

The first step in writing an essay is to get down on paper the ideas you want to include. This writing that you do before you write your essay is called *prewriting*. Look back at the brainstorming you did at the beginning of the project, at the reading passage, and at the notes you took during your group discussions for any ideas that you can use. Since you have already given a lot of thought to this topic, you should have many ideas for your essay.

Brainstorming

Brainstorm for ten minutes on your chosen question. Use a clean sheet of paper to write down your ideas, and write in list form. Leave space between the items in your list so you have room to explore each of your thoughts more. Search your mind for descriptions and explanations that will make your ideas clearer, and add these to your list. Include any examples that might help the reader understand the point you are trying to make. Remember to write down everything that comes to mind. Don't stop to think about whether or not an idea is important or "correct."

After your ten-minute brainstorming, look carefully at your ideas. Think about the essay topic you chose and about your purpose and audience, and cross out any ideas that are irrelevant. If some ideas seem weak or you don't have much to say about them, cross them out, too. If you still have too many ideas to write about in the time available, choose the best ones. If you don't have enough ideas left to write a convincing essay, brainstorm a little longer.

Perhaps you are thinking that all this brainstorming is a waste of time and that it would be better to start directly on your essay so you have more time to write. But the more thinking and prewriting you do now, the easier it will be to write the essay and the better your draft will be. Very few people can think of ideas, organize them clearly in their head, evaluate them, and remember them as they write their essay. So separate the steps. First get your ideas down on paper where you can see them, think about them, and explore them; then concentrate on writing your essay.

Figure 1–1 shows an example of the brainstorming I did for this project. I chose Topic 2. (Note that my list isn't very neat.)

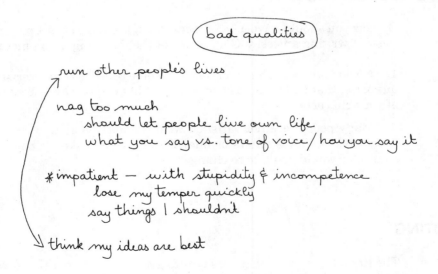

FIGURE 1–1. Example of listing

FIGURE 1–1 continued.

* overly critical
    see people's weaknesses rather than strengths
    admire those who see positive but habit is to see negative

put in CONCLUSION

(never change
  don't get better
  get worse)

* always late
    always rushing — parties, planes, class
    e.g. train in Argentina

spend too much money
love shopping
buy on impulse

bad or good?

high standards
    always think people can do better

WRITING THE FIRST DRAFT

Now you are ready to *write your first draft*. Use ruled, 8½-by-11-inch paper and leave a margin on both the left and right sides of the page. Double-space and write on one side of the paper only. Figure 1–2 shows a sample page.

```
            Project 1: Essay Title        Your Name
            Draft 1

         Xxxxxxxxxxxxxxxxxxxxxxxxxxxxxxxxxxxxxxxx

    xxx.  Xxxxxxxxxxxxxxxxxxxxxxxxxxxxxxxxxxxxxx

    xxxxxxxxxxxxxxxxxxx.  Xxxxxxxxxxxxxxxxxxxxxxx

    xxxxxxxxxxxxxxxxxxxxxxxxxxxxxxxxx.  Xxxxxxxxxx

    xxxxxxxxxxxxxxxxxxxxxxxxx.

            Xxxxxxxxxxxxxxxxxxxxxxxxxxxxxxxxxx.  Xx

    xxxxxxxxxxxxxxxxxxxxxxxxxxxxxxxx.  Xxxxxxxxxxx

    xxxxxxxxxxxxxxx.  Xxxxxxxxxxxxxxxxxxxxxxxxxxxx

    xxxxxxxxxxxxxxxxxxxxxxxxxxxxxxxxxxxxxxxxxxxx.

    Xxxxxxxxxxxxxxxxxxxxxxxxxxxxxxxxxxxxxxxxxxxx.
```

FIGURE 1–2. Sample page

Don't worry about what your essay looks like as long as it is readable. If you change your mind about a word or phrase, or even a whole sentence, just cross it out. Don't worry about grammatical mistakes either. Just concentrate on getting your ideas down on paper as clearly as you can. Your goal is to start using some of the ideas from this project to produce a first draft that you can work with. You will have another opportunity to improve and correct your composition later. If you run out of ideas at any point, try brainstorming again.

When you have finished writing, read your draft from beginning to end. If you want to make any changes, do so. Keep working on your essay until the class period is over. Then clip together your prewriting and draft, and hand them in to your teacher.

BEFORE YOU DO MORE WORK ON YOUR ESSAY, TURN TO THE WRITING SKILLS SECTION BEGINNING ON PAGE 37.

READER RESPONSE

Perhaps you think Draft One is the very best you can do and that there is no way you can improve it. But experienced writers know that their first draft rarely represents what they truly want to say. They know they can make their writing better by rethinking and rewriting.

You, too, can improve your first draft. But to do this requires making judgements about what you have written. It requires deciding whether the words you have put on the paper really express what you want to communicate. It also requires deciding whether or not your reader needs more or different information and how to organize the information better so your reader fully understands you.

There are two methods to help you improve your draft.

1. **Ask someone to read your draft.** Another opinion, from a friend or a teacher, for example, can be valuable. A reader can tell you whether you have really said what you thought you were saying, what parts of your writing are clear and well-organized and what parts are not, and where more information is needed. You can then use these suggestions to help you rethink and rewrite your ideas and improve your essay.

2. **Be your own critical reader.** Most student writers think their teacher is the only possible reader of their work and the only one who can help them improve their draft. But for most of the writing that you will do in your life you won't have a teacher available, and on many occasions (such as essay exams) you won't have any reader at all during the writing process. So you must learn to be your own reader. You must learn to shift from your writer's position to your reader's perspective and look at your own writing as another reader would.

Training yourself to be a constructive reader of your own writing is not easy, but you can start by learning to be a thoughtful and critical reader of someone else's writing. As part of each writing project, therefore, you will exchange drafts with a classmate. You will read your partner's draft and tell him or her what you understand the essay says and how successfully you think it was communicated. Your partner will read your essay and do the same for you. In this way you will help each other to improve your drafts and, even more important, you will help yourself become a better judge of your own writing.

As you read your partner's essay, concentrate on the ideas; don't correct grammar or spelling. That will come later. Right now your task is to let the writer know what you understand and think about the essay—to help the writer see the writing through a reader's eyes.

> In this first project, you are going to focus on a clearly stated main idea and on essay and paragraph unity.

Reader Response Sheet 1

Draft written by _____

Draft read by _____

Read the entire essay. If you can't understand any part, underline it and put a question mark next to it.

Questions to Answer

1. What do you think the writer's purpose is in this essay? (Look back at pages 11–12 if you have forgotten what *purpose* is.) _____

2. What is the writer's main idea? If it is directly stated, underline it and write it here. If there is no statement of the main idea, tell the writer. _____

_____

Is the main idea clearly stated? Do you fully understand it? _____

3. Does the writer's purpose and main idea answer the assignment?

Yes_____ Partly _____ No _____   (If no, give the essay back to the writer.)

Essay and Paragraph Unity

What supporting ideas does the writer give to develop the main idea? Underline the sentence that states each supporting idea and write it below.

1. _____

2. _____

3. _____

4. _____

5. _____

Did you have difficulty stating or understanding any of the supporting ideas?

1. Which ones are not clear? _____

2. Are all the supporting ideas relevant to the main idea?_____

Which ones are not? _____

3. Look at the details or examples the writer gives to illustrate or explain each supporting idea. Are they all relevant; do they really develop that supporting point? _____ Which supporting ideas have irrelevant details?

_____

Essay Form

1. Is the essay divided into appropriate paragraphs? _____

2. Is each paragraph indented? _____

Suggestions for Draft Two

Where would you like more information? Ask the writer three questions.

1. _____

2. _____

3. _____

When you finish, return this response sheet and the draft to the writer.

Example of a Student Essay

Here is Draft One of the essay that a student wrote for this project. (Only the spelling has been corrected.)

A lot of person don't want to say that they have bad qualities. When they talk about themself, they always say the good things about themself.
I am thinking this way too. If somebody ask me to describe myself, I say my good things. But when I sit and think, I think about my bad things. I like to change myself but it doesn't matter how much I try. After few days I am the old Azita that I don't like the bad qualities about.
This time I try to write it down. Maybe it help. First let's start with the worst one. I get angry very easy. Because I am very sensitive person I get upset about the little things. I know the person that I got upset about does not mean anything so I get over it very soon.
The second thing is I am very impatient. I don't like to wait for anything, specially for appointment. I always think that what I am saying is right even when sometimes I am wrong.
The last one is that I am thinking too much about negative things. If I don't pass the test for example. Last week I had a driving test. I am an excellent driver but I was nervous. I don't have self-confidence. But I try to change myself. I hope one day I get perfect.

Azita Abishour

Example of a Reader Response

The following is a Reader Response Sheet that a classmate filled out for Azita after reading her essay.

Questions to Answer

1. What do you think the writer's purpose is in this essay? (Look back at pages 11–12 if you have forgotten what *purpose* is.) *To inform us about herself. To describe herself.*

2. What is the writer's main idea? If it is directly stated, underline it and write it here. If there is no statement of the main idea, tell the writer. *But when I sit and think, I think about my bad things.*

Is the main idea clearly stated? Do you fully understand it? *Yes. But what are things?*

3. Does the writer's purpose and main idea answer the assignment?

Yes __✓__ Partly _____ No _____ (If no, give the essay back to the writer.)

Essay and Paragraph Unity

What supporting ideas does the writer give to develop the main idea? Underline the sentence that states each supporting idea and write it below.

I get angry very easy.

The second thing is I am very impatient.

I always think that what I am saying is right. . . .

The last one is that I am thinking too much about negative things.

Did you have difficulty stating or understanding any of the supporting ideas?

1. Which ones are not clear? *none*

2. Are all the supporting ideas relevant to the main idea? *yes*

Which ones are not? _____

3. Look at the details or examples the writer gives to illustrate or explain each supporting idea. Are they all relevant; do they really develop that supporting point? *no* _____ Which supporting ideas have irrelevant details?

point #1 – the last sentence? point #2 – last sentence is new point, not detail.

Essay Form

1. Is the essay divided into appropriate paragraphs? _no_

2. Is each paragraph indented? _no_

Suggestions for Draft Two

Where would you like more information? Ask the writer three questions.

1. _What little things make you angry?_

2. _What do you do when you are impatient?_

3. _Did you pass your driving test?_

REVISING YOUR DRAFT

The next step in the process is to *revise* your draft. What does *revise* mean? To revise literally means to "re-see" something. Revising is *not*

- finishing your draft because you did not have time earlier.
- just changing a few words or adding a few words.
- correcting your spelling and grammar.
- recopying Draft One more neatly.

To revise means to think again about what you want to say and to rewrite parts or even all of your essay, trying to make your ideas clearer to yourself and your reader.

Revising is not something that just students must do; all good writers, in all languages, revise. The Russian writer Vladimir Nabokov said, "I have re-written—often several times—every word I have ever published. My pencils outlast their erasers." The American author Ernest Hemingway was more blunt. "The first draft of anything," he said, "is shit."

Revision Questions

As you start Draft Two, think about how you looked at your classmate's essay and try to see your own essay in the same way. Look at your reader's comments and suggestions and think about how you might include them. Ask yourself the following questions:

1. *What am I trying to do in this essay? What is my purpose?*

   If you don't know, your reader certainly won't!

2. *Who is going to read my essay? What do my readers need to know to under-stand what I am saying?*

3. *What is the most important idea I want my readers to remember?*

   If your main idea is not clearly stated; try rephrasing it or changing its position. If you have no statement of your main idea, add one.

4. *Are any supporting ideas not closely related to my main idea?*

   Cross out any irrelevant points and, if necessary, add more ideas that are related.

5. *Is each supporting idea clearly stated?*

   If not, add a topic sentence to make the supporting idea clearer. If necessary, rephrase the sentence already there.

6. *Have I discussed each supporting idea in a separate paragraph?*

7. *Are all the details and examples I use to explain each supporting idea closely related to that idea?*

Cross out any irrelevant information and, if necessary, add more details that are related.

WRITING DRAFT TWO

Sometimes even good writers are so dissatisfied with their first draft that they throw it away and start all over again. But more commonly, writers use Draft One as a base for writing Draft Two. They make their changes directly on Draft One.

Revising by Hand

If you write by hand, and double-space your work, you can cross out words and sentences and rewrite them in the margins or in the space above the crossed-out material. In the same way, you can add more information by writing it in the margin or in any empty space, using an arrow to show where it goes. Or you can write a completely new section or paragraph on a separate sheet of paper, and either cut and paste it onto Draft One or mark the section or paragraph so you know where it goes. Don't worry if your draft looks messy. You are the only person who has to read it at this point.

Revising on a Word Processor

If you revise on a word processor, keep a hard copy of Draft One and make changes to Draft One on-screen. Print out a copy periodically so you can see the whole essay and compare it to your first draft.

Judging Your Revision

The problem with most student writers is that they are reluctant to truly revise. So test yourself! When you think you have finished revising, analyze your revision. Compare the new version of your essay to your first draft. Make a list of all the changes you have made. If you find you have not made significant changes, or if you are still not satisfied with your essay, go back and revise some more.

Finally, when you have made all your revisions, decide whether your draft is still readable. If not, write or print out a clean version of Draft Two. Remember to double-space, leave left- and right-hand margins, and write or print on one side of the page only. If you are writing by hand, use standard-size, white, ruled paper. If you are using a typewriter or word processor, use white, unruled bond.

Then clip or staple together Draft Two, your list of revisions, your Reader Response Sheet, Draft One, and your brainstorming—that is, work you have done for all the steps in the writing of your essay. By keeping together all the parts of the project, you have a complete record of how your essay developed.

Example of a Student Revision

After a classmate responded to her first draft, Azita Abishour revised her essay (see Figure 1–3). Note that she made all the changes directly on Draft One.

¶A lot of person don't want to say that they have bad qualities.

When they talk about themself, they always say the good things

about themself. ←

I am thinking this way too. If somebody ask me to describe

myself, I say my good ~~things~~ qualities. But when I sit and think, I think

about my bad things. ~~I like to change myself~~ but it doesn't
                                              B

matter how much I try. After few days I am the old Azita that

I don't like the bad qualities about.

This time I try to write it down. Maybe it help. ¶First let's start

with the worst one. I get angry very easy. Because I am very

For example yesterday my friend said she will call me but she didn't. So I got angry at her.
sensitive person I get upset about the little things. I know the

person that I got upset about does not mean anything so I get
                                                  bad

But get so often angry is waste my energy.
over it very soon. ∧

¶The second thing is I am very impatient. I don't like to wait for

                                    ¶ Also I am very stubborn.
anything, specially for appointment. I always think that what

I am saying is right even when sometimes I am wrong.

¶The last one is that I am thinking too much about negative things.

If I don't pass the test for example. Last week I had a driving

                                    So almost I didn't pass.
test. I am an excellent driver but I was nervous. I don't have

                          many times   But if no, I keep to try.
self-confidence. ~~But~~ I try to change myself. I hope one day I get

perfect.

When I have to wait long time for doctor or dentist I get annoyed.
And sometimes I tell the person what I am thinking.

FIGURE 1–3. Example of revising

After Azita finished, she made a list of her revisions.

1. I put together the first paragraph and half of the second paragraph to make a separate introduction paragraph.

2. I took away the last part of the second paragraph and put it in the conclusion. So the introduction now ends with my main idea.

3. I put an example in the second paragraph and wrote a new last sentence about being angry.

4. I divided the third paragraph into two paragraphs and I gave an example about a little thing which makes me angry.

5. I wrote a new beginning sentence for the new fourth paragraph.

6. I wrote a new conclusion and made a separate paragraph for the conclusion.

*BEFORE YOU DO MORE WORK ON YOUR ESSAY, TURN
TO THE GRAMMAR SECTION ON PAGES 179–195.*

EDITING

Until now, you have been thinking about the content of your essay and its organization. You have been concentrating on making your ideas as clear and convincing to your readers as you could. In the drafts you have written so far, you have been urged not to worry about grammar or spelling because you would have the opportunity to work on them later. Well, now is the time! Now you will work on *editing* your draft. To *edit* means to correct grammar and spelling.

Editing is one of the last steps in writing. Writers edit *after* they have explained and organized their ideas on paper to the best of their ability.

Why Edit?

When you spend so much effort improving your ideas, you want your readers to pay attention to your meaning, not to your mistakes. Writers make mistakes for two reasons. One reason is lack of knowledge. They may not know a grammar rule or how to spell a word. The other reason is carelessness. They may know the rule but simply overlook it.

Obviously, you cannot correct mistakes that you make because of lack of knowledge. Here you will need help from another student or your teacher. As your grammar and spelling skills improve, you will be able to eliminate these errors yourself.

However, mistakes you make out of carelessness are inexcusable. They send a negative message to the reader: "you aren't important enough for me to take the time and effort to correct this piece of writing." Because some readers place a high value on correctness, it is important to eliminate all your careless errors. This requires learning to "sharpen your eye."

Steps in Editing

1. If possible, let some time pass between your writing and editing. By the time you finish revising, you are so involved in the content that it's difficult to concentrate on the form. So let your essay rest for a while before you look for errors.

2. Look for only one type of error at a time. When you try to look for everything at once, you often end up seeing nothing.

3. If you are unsure whether a sentence or phrase is correct, try reading it aloud. If it sounds funny to you, check the form. Consult a grammar book or ask a native speaker. If you think you may have misspelled a word, look it up in the dictionary.

4. Use a pen or pencil that is different in color from the one you used to write your draft. The difference in color makes it easier to see the grammatical corrections you make.

5. Exchange papers with a classmate and edit each other's draft. Because you have no emotional attachment to someone else's writing, it is often easier to spot the grammar and spelling errors. Editing your classmates' papers can help you to sharpen your eye and to learn to see your own grammar and spelling errors more readily.

To guide you in your editing, use the editing checklist on page 35. When you have finished editing, give your entire essay project to your teacher to check the changes and corrections you have made.

When your essay is returned to you, *do not throw it away*. File it in a folder or binder large enough to keep all your writing from this course. You will need all your writing assignments later in the course.

Editing Checklist 1

Draft checked by _____

Read your own essay carefully, looking for and correcting the first kind of error on the list below. Read it a second time to check for the next kind of error. Then read it a third time to check for spelling mistakes. As you finish checking for each type of error, place a check (✔) next to it on the list.

When you finish editing your own essay, exchange papers with a classmate and edit each other's work.

_____ 1.   Basic sentence components

Missing or repeated subject

Missing verb

Missing or repeated object/complement

_____ 2.   Verbs

Wrong verb tense

Wrong verb form

_____ 3.   Spelling (*Hint*: To check spelling, read each line of words from right to left. This will help you see each word individually.)

Teacher's comments: _____

_____

_____

_____

_____

When you finish editing, attach this sheet to your draft.

WRITING SKILLS: UNDERSTANDING PARAGRAPH AND ESSAY STRUCTURE

Looking at a Paragraph

You have all heard the word *paragraph*, and you all have in your mind some definition of what this word means. But let's look more closely at what a paragraph is.

The following paragraph is from an essay titled "A Few Kind Words for Envy" by Joseph Epstein. In the essay he describes the different kinds of envy or jealousy he has felt in his life.

° **a very great deal:** very, very much

° **stack up next to:** be equal to

° **for openers:** slang for *to begin*

° **pretty hot stuff:** very special

° **spikes:** shoes with metal points on the soles to prevent slipping

° **Roy Rogers:** a famous movie cowboy

° **flowing-maned:** long haired (A mane is the neck hair on a horse.)

° **palomino:** a kind of horse

To begin my life not quite with the beginning of my life, the first thing I can remember envying was the parents of two boys I grew up with named Sammy and Billy Cowling. I loved my parents a very great deal,° you understand, but on paper they just didn't stack up next to° the Cowlings' parents. For openers,° their father, Sam Cowling, Sr., was on the radio; he was the comedian on a then immensely popular radio show called *The Breakfast Club*. . . . Even at five years old, I knew that being on the radio was pretty hot stuff.° He also happened to be a friendly man, kindly and thoughtful to children, and a good athlete. Sam Cowling, Sr., owned baseball spikes.° I knew of no other father who owned spikes. Mrs. Cowling was feminine, beautifully so, and named Dale, which was the name of Roy Rogers's° wife. The Cowlings seemed so wondrous to me as a child that, in those days, I shouldn't have been surprised to learn that they kept a flowing-maned° palomino° in the dining room of their two-bedroom apartment. I don't want anyone to think that I envied the Cowling kids so much that I would have traded my own [parents for theirs]. I would never finally have done that, but before deciding not to do it, I believe I would have had to give it considerable thought.

1. What has the writer done to show you that this is a paragraph?

    _____

2. Look at the ideas in the paragraph. Has the writer included ideas that have no relation to each other? Or is there one idea that runs through the whole passage, one idea that all the sentences in the paragraph describe, explain, or illustrate?

    _____

    If so, underline the sentence that tells you this idea. Write it here. _____

    _____

    Where is it placed in the passage? _____

What Is a Paragraph?

A *paragraph* is a unit of thought. It is a group of sentences that logically develops one idea. The single idea that all the sentences of the paragraph develop is called the *main idea* of the paragraph. All the information included in the paragraph serves to illustrate, explain, or describe the main idea.

In most academic writing, the main idea of the paragraph is usually stated directly in a *topic sentence*. The topic sentence can appear anywhere in the paragraph, but generally it comes at or near the beginning of the paragraph.

In literary writing, however, the main idea of a paragraph is often not stated directly in a topic sentence but is implied. The reader can still understand what it is by reading the paragraph.

To show the beginning of a paragraph, the writer *indents*. To *indent* means to start the first line of the paragraph a short distance away from the margin. Indenting leaves a blank space between the left-hand margin and the first word; all remaining lines of the paragraph start directly at the left-hand margin. Notice how the paragraphs on this page are indented and that you can clearly see where each paragraph begins. When writing by hand, most writers indent about three-quarters of an inch. When typing, five spaces is the standard indention.

A paragraph can form a complete passage all by itself. More commonly, however, a paragraph is part of a larger text (such as an essay, an article, or a book) and presents one smaller, more specific idea of a larger, more general idea.

How Long Is a Paragraph?

Paragraphs vary in length. A paragraph can run a whole page or more, or can consist of only one sentence or even just a phrase. But more commonly, a modern English paragraph has three to ten related sentences, or about 50 to 250 words.

The best examples of how long English paragraphs should be can be found by looking at good writing. Every time you read, look at the paragraphs. For example, how long is the paragraph on page 37? What about the paragraphs in the reading passage on pages 16–17?

Looking at an Essay

Now let's think about an essay. All of you have heard the word *essay*, but perhaps you are not really sure what the term means. The passage below is an example of an essay. It is titled "Recipe for an Atheist" and was written by Laura Waterbury when she was a senior in an American high school. What is it that makes this an essay? Think about how many ideas the writer is trying to communicate to you. Are there many different ideas collected together or is there one central idea that runs through the whole composition?

° **atheist:** a person who does not believe in the existence of God

° **secular:** not religious

I am an atheist.° I have always been an atheist and I can't foresee ever being anything but an atheist.

I did not experience something that revealed to me that God did not exist. I did not undergo some sort of revelation that changed the basis for all of my beliefs. I was brought up in a secular° household with intellectual parents who believed only what could be supported by evidence. They passed that way of looking at the world to both their children. Of the two of us, my brother always related more to the religion of my mother's family,

° Passover: a Jewish holiday celebrating freedom from slavery
° great-aunt: the sister of a grandparent
° Hanukkah: a Jewish holiday celebrating freedom of religious expression

Judaism. But the Passover° dinners I spent at my great-aunt's,° and the lighting of the Hanukkah° candles at my grandmother's never meant anything more to me than family get-togethers and opening presents.

I never thought about my atheism, or even considered it out of the ordinary until I was eight. I had thought that not believing in God was common and widely accepted; it was like my belief that everyone had a passport just because I had always had one. I remember I was sitting in class. It was the fourth grade, the first of the two years that I spent living in Ecuador. I was surrounded by a group of girls, all of whom accompanied their parents to church every Sunday. They were all talking about God and, as I usually do, I opened my big mouth. They couldn't understand the concept of God not existing, nor do I think they had ever met anyone who believed that. I remember what they told me. They said, "Well, if you don't believe in God, then you're going to go to hell." That would have scared any child right into God's hands, including me, but my best friend Patricia piped up° and saved me from doubting my doubt. She said, "But if she doesn't believe in hell, how can she go there?" And I thought to myself, "Yeah, that's right." Now when I look back to that time, I realize what an intelligent thing she said, especially for an eight year old.

° piped up: began to speak, especially in a high voice

° trade in: give away in part-payment for something else

Although the idea of going to hell if I don't trade in° my beliefs no longer scares me, Patricia's answer is the one I always use when someone says something like what those girls said to me years ago. Also since then I have re-evaluated my belief that no one cares if I am an atheist or not and have kept my mouth closed in certain situations. I have at times even questioned my belief as all people do at one point or another. But after each moment of doubt, I have become more firm and certain that what I believe is true. I am not ashamed to be an atheist; rather I am proud. I am proud not only because I feel it to be the truth, but also because unlike many of the people I know I have actually come to a conclusion about God and am willing to live with the consequences of that conclusion.

I feel that as an atheist I am more accepting of different religions. I find myself extremely tolerant of other people's beliefs because their laws cannot challenge my own, seeing as there are no laws that an atheist must follow. At the same time, I do not preach° atheism because I do not believe it is something that can be imposed,° only something that can be learned for oneself.

° preach: urge others to accept something that you believe in
° imposed: forced on people

Many of my friends ask if it's depressing to constantly know that the life I have now is all I will ever have. My answer is a definite "No." On the contrary, it shows me that I have no time for depression. This is the only chance at life I'll ever get, so I'd better make something of myself now rather than later.

1. Is this composition about one idea or does it discuss many different ideas?

_____

2. Can you find a sentence where the writer specifically tells you this idea? Underline it and write it here. _____

_____

Where is it placed in the passage? _____

3. Is this idea a statement of fact or a generally accepted truth, or is it the writer's personal view or opinion? _____

4. Can you divide this composition into sections? How many do you find?

_____ What is the purpose of each section? _____

_____

What Is an Essay?

An *essay* is a series of paragraphs about one idea. The one idea that is central to the whole essay is called the *main idea*. The main idea of an essay is a statement of the writer's thoughts or opinion about a topic. The word essay comes from the French word *essai* meaning an attempt or a try. Thus, the writer of an essay tries to communicate his or her point of view on a subject, to express his or her outlook or personal ideas about a subject.[1]

Most essays include a clear and direct statement of the main idea at or close to the beginning of the essay. This is especially true of academic essays. However, even in academic writing, if the main idea is very controversial or if the writer wants to build an argument first or create suspense, the main idea may not be stated until the end. And in some essays, especially literary essays, there may be no explicit statement of the main idea at all, and the readers are left to infer this idea on their own.

How Long Is an Essay?

Like a paragraph, there is no predetermined length to an essay. Rarely is it less than one typed page or more than twenty or twenty-five pages. Within that range, however, the length is determined by whom you are writing for, how much time you have to write, how complex your subject is, and how much you need to say to develop your main idea in a convincing way. Again, reading is the best teacher of writing.

Parts of an Essay

Most essays can be divided into three sections. The first part is the *introduction*. The introduction consists of one or more paragraphs that tell the reader what the essay will be about. It usually also contains a statement of the main idea. The second part of the essay is called the *body*. It is the longest section and contains the information that supports and develops the main idea. If the body includes several different supporting ideas, each is usually presented in one or more separate paragraphs. Finally, the essay ends with one or more paragraphs of *conclusion*.

This division, however, is not universal. As you read, you will notice that sometimes an essay writer will jump right into the body with little or no introduction.

Look back at the essay on pages 38–39. How is it divided?

------

[1]A piece of writing that primarily presents factual information without any statement of the author's own opinion or position is more correctly called a *report*.

Paragraphing

Writers use paragraphs to show readers what ideas are important, what ideas are more closely related, and where one thought unit ends and a new one begins. In academic writing, the breaks between thought units are often clearer and there is more agreement about where the paragraph divisions should fall. In literary writing, however, thought units are not always as obvious and even native speakers may disagree about where paragraphs should be divided.

To give you practice in thinking about paragraphing, read the following essay that a student wrote for this project. All the paragraph divisions have been removed. Decide where you think divisions should occur and mark the beginning of each paragraph with the paragraph symbol ¶.

1   The event in my life that affected me in an important way was an
2   operation on my leg. I was twenty years old, and I was a very good rugby
3   player in my country, but I had a big problem with my leg which affected my
4   performance on the team. I couldn't run very fast because I had an
5   infection in my right leg. The team doctor told me that I had to undergo an
6   operation if I wanted to keep on playing. Thinking of my health and the
7   future of my athletic life, I followed the doctor's directions, even though I
8   didn't like the idea of going to the hospital. I just thought of my future life
9   in rugby when I made the decision. After the operation, I started to think
10   about people who for different reasons were unable to walk by themselves.
11   I mean people who maybe had broken a leg or people with a stretched
12   tendon. These are things that you can always see in people who play
13   rugby. For them, trying to walk just ten yards is like walking one hour for a
14   person that doesn't have that problem. Suddenly I was in the same
15   position as these people. I couldn't walk by myself. When I woke up in the
16   morning I had to call my father or mother to ask them to help me go to
17   the bathroom. That was embarrassing, but I had to do it. If I wished to go
18   up or down the stairs, I had to do it jumping on one leg because I had to
19   keep my operated leg off the floor. Also when I went to sleep, I had to keep
20   my leg hanging over the edge of the bed all night. I couldn't move my body
21   even a little. These problems maybe sound funny, but the truth was I felt
22   very bad because I couldn't do many basic things by myself. Because of
23   this operation, I began to value the most simple things like walking, going
24   up and down stairs, taking a bus, or sleeping like a normal person. I
25   started to be more careful and to think about each step I made. I started
26   to understand how fragile the human body is. I'll never forget this event.
27   It was one of the most terrible things that happened to me in rugby, but it
28   was one of the most valuable in my life.

Jorge Cohen

WRITING SKILLS: THE CONCEPT OF UNITY

Judging the Relationship of Ideas in a Paragraph

Since a paragraph discusses only one idea, all its thoughts, explanations, and examples must be connected to that idea. The main idea of the paragraph controls the paragraph; it determines what other ideas are related or relevant and can be included.

Look at the following short essay, "Why I Decided to Come to This College." As you read it, think about how successful the writer has been in maintaining the one-idea rule of English paragraphs. Specifically, think about whether each paragraph has a single controlling idea and how closely the details of each paragraph are related to that idea.

1There are a lot of reasons why I decided to come to this college.

2First, my sister told me this is a very good school and the teachers are very good also. She knows this because she used to come here. The area is really nice and the college is very close to my home.

3The people here are very nice. One time I came to the college because I wanted to see how it was. I saw that students tried to help each other. I didn't know English very well, but somebody guided me and told me what I had to do. Since I am a new student, I want a school where people are friendly.

4Also, the college is very close to my home and my job. I only have to take one bus to get home and to the place that I work. It takes me 20 minutes to get there so I spend only a little time traveling. I have a friend who lives on the same street as me, but she goes to another college far away. She has to take a subway and a bus. Every day it takes her an hour and a half to get there or come back home. In addition to time, she has to spend a lot of money. Every time I see her she complains about that. If I ride on the subways, when I get off I get a headache; then I can't think well and I am angry. I just want to come home. That's a good reason to find a college near my home.

5Now I am very happy that I decided to come to this school.

1. Look closely at the first body paragraph (para. 2). Does it discuss just one idea? _____

2. Reread the second body paragraph (para. 3). Does it discuss just one idea? _____What is the topic sentence? _____

_____

Are all the details in the paragraph closely related to the idea expressed in the topic sentence? _____

3.   Now look at the last body paragraph (para. 4). Does it discuss just one idea? _____What is the topic sentence? _____

_____

Are all the details in the paragraph closely related to the idea expressed in the topic sentence? _____ *(Hint:* look especially carefully at the discussion of the subway.)

Judging the Relationship of Ideas in an Essay

The same concept of one idea applies to an English essay. When you write an essay, it is very important to restrict your discussion to one idea, the main idea of the essay. This main idea controls all the other ideas in the essay. It determines what other information is relevant and sets limits on what other thoughts can be included in the essay.

The main idea of an essay is like a promise to the reader about what the essay will be about. English readers expect the writer to fulfill this promise. If the writer goes off in a different direction and discusses something else, the reader will be confused.

The following is another student essay. After each paragraph is a question to help you evaluate how successful the writer has been in sticking to the main idea and fulfilling the promise to the reader.

If I could change something about myself, I would do one thing. I would change my weight.

Underline the writer's main idea. What do you expect the rest of the essay to be about? _____

When I arrived in New York, my weight was 100 pounds. I thought, "I have to take care of myself. Nobody will worry about my health like my mother, so I have to gain weight a little bit in order to keep my body healthy."

Does this paragraph support the main idea of the essay? _____

But now I am getting to be a big eater. My weight has become 110 pounds in only two weeks. So it is harder to do anything than before. I'm a sluggish woman now! I want to change my size immediately and I will try to go back to my shape as soon as possible.

Does this paragraph support the main idea of the essay? _____

However, I would not change anything except my size. My name was given by my parents whom I love very much. I think they spent a lot of time to find my name. So I appreciate it and I've never thought to change my name.

Does this paragraph support the main idea of the essay? _____

How about my age? I would not change it because I have a policy not to regret anything about my life. Life is just once. Even if I can go back to 18, 19 years old, or even if I can skip my age, I don't want to do it. I'm enjoying now, right now!

Does this paragraph support the main idea of the essay? _____

That's why I prefer not to change anything about me except my weight.

Is this the same idea that the writer started out with at the beginning of the essay? _____

Maintaining Paragraph and Essay Unity

In English, a well-written paragraph or essay has a feature called *unity*. That is, all the thoughts in the passage explicitly relate to the main idea. Readers expect the writer to "stick to the subject," to carry out the promise of the main idea. Thus, in a unified essay the point of each supporting paragraph relates directly and closely to the main idea of the essay, and in each supporting paragraph, all the information relates directly and closely to the main idea of the paragraph. If the writing contains any information that is not obviously related, the essay lacks unity.

This requirement of unity sometimes causes student writers problems. Why? Sometimes writers feel they must fill the page with words, so they include every detail they can think of even when those details are not relevant. Or sometimes writers forget what they are writing about or change their mind and go off in a different direction halfway through their essay. Or sometimes information that appears unrelated may actually be relevant, but the writer has not made the relationship obvious to the reader.

These are problems all writers must deal with. But non-native speakers of English have an additional problem in judging unity: deciding *what information is considered relevant*?

Every language is different. What English-speaking readers consider related information is not necessarily the same as what readers who speak other languages accept. Specifically, there are two characteristics of unity in English that may be different from those in your native language.

First, because it is more direct than many other languages, English sets narrower limits than most languages on what ideas can be included. It views as relevant only information that is very closely related to the main idea. Or to put it another way, the controlling idea in English controls very tightly.

Also unlike many languages, English demands that the connections between ideas be obvious. It is the writer's job to show how ideas are related whereas other languages leave the task of making connections to the reader.

So what can you do to improve the unity of your writing? First, remember that English is different from your own language and try to look more critically at what ideas you include. If you have any American friends who you think are good writers, ask them to look at your writing and tell you if any of your ideas seem irrelevant. And above all, every time you read, look at the kind of information the writer has chosen to include in the work as a whole and in each individual paragraph. Continued practice as a reader and writer will help you learn to judge the unity of your own writing.

SUGGESTED JOURNAL TOPICS

1. What's on My Mind Right Now?

2. Emily Dickinson was an American poet who lived in Amherst, Massachusetts, from 1830–1886. She wrote the following poem around 1861.

> I'm nobody! Who are you?
> Are you—Nobody—Too?
> Then there's a pair of us?
> Don't tell! They'd advertise—you know!

° **dreary:** depressing, sad
° **livelong:** entire, whole
° **bog:** soft, wet area; swamp (where frogs live)

> How dreary°—to be—Somebody!
> How public—like a Frog—
> To tell one's name—the livelong° June—
> To an admiring Bog!°

Are you a nobody or a somebody? Which would you rather be?

3. My Reflection in the Mirror

4. Memories of My Childhood

5. Here is Garfield the cat discussing one of his pet peeves. What is your pet peeve?

Garfield reprinted by permission of USF, Inc.

6. If I could be reincarnated, I would choose to come back as . . .

7. At the age of eighty-five, Bernard Baruch, a famous American statesman, said, "To me old age is always fifteen years older than I am." What is old age to you?

8. Choose a color that best describes you and explain why.

9. What Makes Me Angry?

10. Russell Baker is a well-known American writer who writes a weekly newspaper column. Most of his work is light-hearted and humorous. Here is part of an article he wrote about himself.

° **Depression-generation:** people born during the Great Depression, a period of high unemployment which began in 1929 and lasted through most of the 1930s

° **hearing-impaired:** unable to hear well

I am a European-American.

I am a male European-American.

I am a Depression-generation,° male European-American.

I am a hearing-impaired,° Depression-generation, male European-American.

I am a college-educated, hearing-impaired, Depression-generation, male European-American

Because I have not lost significant amounts of hair, I am not a bald, college-educated, hearing-impaired, Depression-generation, male European-American. Instead, I am a comb-carrying, college-educated, hearing-impaired, Depression-generation, male European-American.

I am a heterosexual, comb-carrying, college-educated, hearing-impaired, Depression-generation, male European-American.

Because I am married, I am not a single, heterosexual, comb-carrying, college-educated, hearing-impaired, Depression-generation, male European-American.

Instead, I am a married, heterosexual, comb-carrying, college-educated, hearing-impaired, Depression-generation, male European-American.

° **shun:** avoid; keep away from

° **square:** slang for old-fashioned

° **poverty line:** the point at which the government considers you poor

° **David Letterman:** a television talk-show host and comedian

° **comparatively financially disadvantaged:** economically less successful compared to others

[Because I cannot] understand . . . rock music, I shun° it. . . . Therefore, I am a square,° married, heterosexual, comb-carrying, college-educated, hearing-impaired, Depression-generation, male European-American.

Though I am not . . . below the official Government poverty line,° when pondering David Letterman's° $14 million salary and the $1 million salary of the average . . . baseball player, I realize that neither am I doing so well in the money department.

In short, I am a comparatively financially disadvantaged,° square, married, heterosexual, comb-carrying, college-educated, hearing-impaired, Depression-generation, male European-American.

Using the same style of writing, how would you describe yourself?

11. The Best Birthday Present Someone Could Give Me

12. If I could change something about myself, I would change . . .

13. In the following excerpt, the American actor, movie director, and writer Woody Allen recalls his childhood career as a dreidel player. A dreidel is a small, four-sided top that Jewish children play with at holiday time. It has different letters on each of its four sides and children bet which letter will be face up when the dreidel stops spinning and falls over.

° **hustler:** a person who persuades by deceit
° **contrived:** succeeded in doing something in spite of its difficulty
° **waxing:** growing
° **pool:** billiards
° **shark:** someone who is clever at getting money from others in dishonest ways
° **stakes:** money that can be won
° **gutted:** without money
° **muttering:** complaining in a low voice
° **Legs Diamond and Dutch Schultz:** famous gamblers during Prohibition
° **felt:** type of cloth that covers a pool table
° **smart:** fashionable
° **cleaning up:** winning

Confessions of a hustler.° At ten I hustled dreidel. I practiced endlessly spinning the little lead top and could make the letters come up in my favor more often than not. After that I mercilessly contrived° to play dreidel with kids and took their money.

"Let's play for two cents," I'd say, my eyes waxing° wide and innocent like a big-time pool° shark's.° Then I'd lose the first game deliberately. After, I'd move the stakes° up. Four cents, maybe six, maybe a dime. Soon the other kid would find himself en route home, gutted° and muttering.° Dreidel hustling got me through the fifth grade. I often had visions of myself turning pro. I wondered if when I got older I could play my generation's equivalent of Legs Diamond° or Dutch Schultz° for a hundred thousand a game. I saw myself bathed in won money, sitting around a green felt° table or getting off great trains, my best dreidel in a smart° carrying case as I went from city to city looking for action, always cleaning up,° always drinking bourbon, always taking care of my precious manicured spinning hand.

Write your own childhood "confession."

14. I think it's hard: to apologize

to save money

to arrive on time

to refuse dessert

What's hard for you? Make your own list of at least fifteen items.

15. Clark Blaise is a Canadian writer who lives in the United States. His father was French-Canadian; his wife is Indian. In the following paragraph, he describes the dualities in his life.

° **Quebecois:** a person from the province of Quebec, Canada, who speaks French and supports French-Canadian culture

Sociologically, I am an American. Psychologically, a Canadian. Sentimentally, a Quebecois.° By marriage, part of the Third World. My passport says Canadian, but I was born in America; my legal status says immigrant. Resident Alien. Everywhere I see dualities.

What are the dualities in your life?

16. Which would you rather be: healthy, wealthy, or wise?

17. In an article called "Unachievers," Russell Baker described himself as "the man you'd most hate to spend a long weekend with." In the following excerpt, he gives some of his reasons.

Besides not playing golf, tennis, squash, volleyball, polo, water polo, softball, hardball, two-hand touch, basketball, hopscotch, jacks, croquet and Scrabble, I did not dive off the high board, jump fences on horseback, hike, camp, work out on the weight machine, fish, hunt or listen to police calls on shortwave radio.

When people said, "Try my new $240,000 Italo-Teutonic sports car with the Simplexiconic transmission that goes from here to there in tenths of fractionated seconds," I said, "I can't drive a car with a manual gear shift."

When people said, "Just send a fax," I said, "I don't fax." I didn't dare speak the truth, saying, "I'm afraid to fax because I don't know how to fax, and I'm afraid if I try to fax I'll hit the wrong button and wipe out all of Fax World . . ."

What can you *not* do?

18. The Last Time I Cried

19. Margaret Atwood is one of Canada's leading writers. She wrote the following poem, "This Is a Photograph of Me."

It was taken some time ago.
At first it seems to be
a smeared°
print: blurred° lines and grey flecks°
blended with the paper;

Then, as you scan°
it, you see in the left-hand corner
a thing that is like a branch: part of a tree
(balsam or spruce) emerging
and, to the right, halfway up
what ought to be a gentle
slope,° a small frame house.

In the background there is a lake,
and beyond that, some low hills.

The photograph was taken
the day after I drowned.°

I am in the lake, in the center
of the picture, just under the surface.

It is difficult to say where
precisely, or to say
how large or small I am:
the effect of water on light is a distortion°

but if you look long enough,
eventually
you will be able to see me.

° **smeared:** rubbed so the images blend
° **blurred:** unclear
° **flecks:** very small spots

° **scan:** look closely at every part of, search

° **slope:** hill

° **drowned:** died in water

° **distortion:** twisted out of its usual shape

Find a photograph of yourself and paste it in your journal. What does this photo say about you and your life?

20. "Everyone is a moon, and has a dark side which he never shows to anybody" (Mark Twain). Describe your dark side.

ADDITIONAL WRITING TOPICS

1.   Write pages 127-129 of your autobiography. Decide what period or specific event(s) in your life these pages cover and focus only on that time or that experience.

2.   How have experiences shaped your life? Describe an event in your life that affected you in some significant way, and discuss how you have become a different person as a result of this experience. (Note that this assignment has two parts. First, describe the event, something that happened to you or something you saw or did. Second, discuss how this experience influenced or changed you as a person.)

3.   Reread the passage by Richard Rodriguez on pages 16–17. As a young teenager, did you have a similar experience? Was there anything about your body or appearance that bothered you?

4.   Many universities, as part of their admissions requirements, ask students to write an essay about themselves that will help the school judge their application. Write an essay for the admissions office of this school to help them learn more about you. Tell them about some ability or characteristic that you possess or some experience that you have had that would make you an asset to this institution. (*Note:* The essay by Laura Waterbury on pages 38–39 was written for this purpose.)

ADDITIONAL READINGS

Russell Baker. "My Lack of Gumption." *Growing Up*. Chapter 2, pp. 9–17. New York: Congdon & Weed 1982.

Nora Ephron. "A Few Words About Breasts: Shaping Up Absurd." *Crazy Salad: Some Things About Women*. Alfred A. Knopf 1972. Reprinted in *A Writer's Reader,* 6th ed. edited by Donald Hall and D. L. Emblem. HarperCollins 1991. Also reprinted in *Life Studies: A Thematic Reader*, 3rd ed. Edited by David Cavitch. New York: St. Martin's Press 1989.

Terry Galloway. "I'm Listening as Hard as I Can." *Texas Monthly:* April 1981. Reprinted in *Life Studies: A Thematic Reader,* 3rd ed. Edited by David Cavitch. New York: St. Martin's Press 1989.

Look at autobiographies that are self-reflective. Here are three suggestions.

Bebe Moore Campbell. *Sweet Summer: Growing Up With and Without My Dad*. New York: Ballantine Books 1989.

Edward T. Hall. *An Anthropology of Everyday Life: An Autobiography*. New York: Anchor Books 1992.

Jake Lamar. *Bourgeois Blues*. Plume Books 1991.

P R O J E C T
2
THINKING ABOUT WRITING

In this project, you will

- practice another way of writing down your ideas about a subject when you brainstorm: free-writing.
- think about the difference between general ideas and specific ideas.
- look at different ways writers develop their ideas.
- practice developing your own ideas more fully.
- write several assignments about the topic of writing.
- work on critical reading and revision again.
- continue to practice editing your writing.
- continue writing in your journal.

GETTING IDEAS

In the previous project, you practiced listing as a way of writing down ideas for an essay. As you brainstormed about the topic—as you let your mind wander freely in search of ideas—you listed whatever thoughts came to your mind. Making a list of your ideas is a very useful way to start recording your thoughts about a topic. But it isn't the only way.

Brainstorming Method 2: Free-writing

Another method for getting your ideas onto paper before you start an essay is *free-writing*. In this form of brainstorming, you write in sentences, and the sentences follow one after another. However, in free-writing, just as in listing, grammatical correctness is not important. Nor is it necessary to organize your ideas or think about main ideas or paragraphs. Just write whatever ideas come to mind in whatever order you think of them. Your goal is to start your ideas flowing and to begin to get them down on paper so you can see them and consider them.

Actually, this method should be familiar to you because you have already done some free-writing in your journal. However, in your journal, free-writing is an end in itself. As a brainstorming technique, it is just a beginning.

The following paragraph is an example of free-writing that a student did for this project.

My writing history isn't yet finished; probably I have to learn yet the right method to have a good writing style. Or maybe I will never be a good writer. All that I know about writing, I have learned it during my school age. I remember we had a very strict teacher who was very exigent and she expected much from us. But I swear to have never been a good writer. It was very hard for me to write a long essay. I preferred the sinthesis to the analysis and the oral way to the write method. I remember yet my anxiety when we had to make, once a month, our writen composition in the class. The teacher always gave us two different topics: one about Italian literature and other about actuality. I always chose the actuality topic because I was more interested about the life's events. When I was twelve years old, I started a relation with a french girl, so I began to write to her long and . . . . letters. At the beginning, it was very hard for me to put down on the paper everything I had in my head. But later it was easier.

Alessandro Caggia

For this project you are going to try free-writing as a way of writing down your ideas.

STARTING TO THINK ABOUT THE TOPIC OF THIS PROJECT

Think about writing in general and specifically about your own history as a writer in your native language. Think about your childhood and your years in school, about how and where you learned to write, and what you wrote. Using the space provided below, brainstorm for ten minutes on "My Writing History."

_____

_____

_____

_____

_____

_____

_____

_____

_____

_____

_____

_____

_____

_____

_____

_____

_____

_____

_____

Getting Ideas through Reading

1.   Do you always speak the same way? Do you talk to your parents or teachers the same way you talk to your friends? When you write, do you always write the same way? Do your letters to friends sound the same as your school compositions?

2.   Musically and artistically talented people can usually be recognized when they are very young. Math geniuses, too, can usually be identified early in life. But what about good writers? Are there any really good child writers? If you aren't a good writer when you are young, can you become one?

3.   Did any teacher ever tell you that you were not good at writing? Did anyone ever tell you that you should avoid courses that require good language skills and study math and science or engineering instead?

Amy Tan is an Asian-American author whose writing is based on her experiences growing up in a Chinese family in California. In this essay titled "Mother Tongue" (*mother tongue* means native language), she talks about how the English that she heard at home influenced both her decision to become a writer and her style of writing. The passage below is a shorter version of the original essay.

I am a writer. And by that definition, I am someone who has always loved language. I am fascinated by language in daily life. I spend a great deal of my time thinking about the power of language—the way it can evoke° an emotion, a visual image, a complex idea, or a simple truth. Language is the tool of my trade.° And I use them all—all the Englishes I grew up with.

° **evoke:** produce, bring to the surface
° **trade:** work

Recently, I was made keenly aware of the different Englishes I do use. I was giving a talk to a large group of people, the same talk I had already given to half a dozen other groups. The nature of the talk was about my writing, my life, and my book, *The Joy Luck Club*. The talk was going along well enough, until I remembered one major difference that made the whole talk sound wrong. My mother was in the room. And it was perhaps the first time she had heard me give a lengthy speech, using the kind of English I have never used with her. I was saying things like, "The intersection of memory upon imagination" and "There is an aspect of my fiction that relates to thus-and-thus"—a speech filled with carefully wrought° grammatical phrases, burdened,° it suddenly seemed to me, with nominalized° forms, past perfect tenses, conditional phrases, all the forms of standard English that I had learned in school and through books, the forms of English I did not use at home with my mother.

° **wrought:** constructed (old word)
° **burdened:** made heavy
° **nominalized:** word in noun form

Just last week, I was walking down the street with my mother, and I again found myself conscious of the English I was using, the English I do use with her. We were talking about the price of new and used furniture and I heard myself saying this: "Not waste money that way." My husband was with us as well, and he didn't notice any switch in my English. And then I realized why. It's because over the twenty years we've been together I've often used that same kind of English with him, and sometimes he even uses it with me. It has become our language of intimacy,° a different sort of English that relates to family talk, the language I grew up with.

° **intimacy:** closeness, privacy

So you'll have some idea of what this family talk I heard sounds like, I'll quote what my mother said during a recent conversation which I video-taped and then transcribed.° During this conversation, my mother was talking about a political gangster° in Shanghai who had the same last name as her family's, Du, and how the gangster in his early years wanted to be adopted by her family, which was rich by comparison. Later, the gangster became more powerful, far richer than my mother's family, and one day showed up at my mother's wedding to pay his respects. Here's what she said in part:

° **transcribed:** wrote down something recorded
° **gangster:** a member of a group of criminals

"Du Yusong having business like fruit stand. Like off the street kind. He is Du like Du Zong—but not Tsung-ming Island people. The local people call putong, like river east side, he belong to that side local people. That man want to ask Du Zong father take him in like become own family. Du Zong father wasn't look down on him, but didn't take seriously, until that man big like become a mafia. Now important person, very hard to inviting him. Chinese way, came only to show respect, don't stay for dinner. Respect for making big celebration, he shows up. Mean gives lots of respect. Chinese custom. Chinese social life that way. If too important won't have to stay too long. He come to my wedding. I didn't see, I heard it. I gone to boy's side, they have YMCA dinner. Chinese age I was nineteen."

. . . Some of my friends tell me they understand 50 percent of what my mother says. Some say they understand 80 to 90 percent. Some say they understand none of it, as if she were speaking pure Chinese. But to me, my mother's English is perfectly clear, perfectly natural. It's my mother tongue. Her language, as I hear it, is vivid,° direct, full of observation and imagery.° That was the language that helped shape the way I saw things, expressed things, made sense of the world.

. . . Like others, I have described [the kind of English my mother speaks] as "broken" or "fractured" English. But I wince° when I say that. It has always bothered me that I can think of no way to describe it other than "broken," as if it were damaged and needed to be fixed, as if it lacked a certain wholeness and soundness.° I've heard other terms used, "limited English," for example. But they seem just as bad. . . .

. . . Sociologists° and linguists° probably will tell you that a person's developing language skills are more influenced by peers. But I do think that the language spoken in the family, especially in immigrant families which are more insular,° plays a large role in shaping the language of the child. And I believe that [my mother's English] affected my results on achievement tests, IQ° tests, and the SAT.° While my English skills were never judged as poor, compared to math, English could not be considered my strong suit.° In grade° school I did moderately well, getting perhaps Bs, sometimes B-pluses, in English and scoring perhaps in the sixtieth or seventieth percentile on achievement tests. But those scores were not good enough to override° the opinion that my true abilities lay in math and science, because in those areas I achieved As and scored in the ninetieth percentile or higher.

. . . I have been thinking about all this lately, about my mother's English, about achievement tests. Because lately I've been asked, as a writer, why there are not more Asian Americans represented in American literature. Why are there few Asian Americans enrolled in creative writing programs? Why do so many Chinese students go into engineering? Well, these are broad sociological questions I can't begin to answer. But I have noticed . . . that Asian students, as a whole, always do significantly better on math achievement tests than in English. And this makes me think that there are other Asian-American students whose English spoken in the home might also be described as "broken" or "limited." And perhaps they also have teachers who are steering° them away from writing and into math and science, which is what happened to me.

Fortunately, I happen to be rebellious in nature and enjoy the challenge of disproving assumptions° made about me. I became an English major my first year in college, after being enrolled as pre-med.° I started writing non-fiction as a freelancer° the week after I was told by my former boss that writing was my worst skill and I should hone° my talents toward account management.

But it wasn't until 1985 that I finally began to write fiction. And at first I wrote using what I thought to be wittily° crafted° sentences, sentences that would finally prove I had mastery over the English language. Here's an example. . . . "That was my mental quandary° in its nascent° state." A terrible line, which I can barely pronounce.

Fortunately . . . I later decided I should envision a reader for the stories I would write. And the reader I decided upon was my mother, because these were stories about mothers. So with this reader in mind—and in fact she did read my early drafts—I began to write stories using all the Englishes I grew up with: the English I spoke to my mother, which for lack of a better term might be described as "simple"; the English she used with me, which

---

° **vivid:** bright, colorful
° **imagery:** pictures in the mind

° **wince:** to move slightly away from something unpleasant

° **soundness:** good condition

° **sociologist:** person who studies society and social behavior
° **linguist:** person who studies the science of language
° **insular:** like an island, isolated
° **IQ:** intelligence
° **SAT:** Scholastic Aptitude Test, given to high school seniors who wish to attend college
° **suit:** ability
° **grade:** elementary
° **override:** outweigh, steering: directing

° **steering:** directing

° **assumption:** something taken to be true without proof
° **pre-med:** undergraduate program for students who want to attend medical school
° **freelancer:** person who sells work to any employer (rather than just working for one employer)
° **hone:** sharpen
° **wittily:** cleverly
° **crafted:** made, constructed
° **quandary:** dilemma; feeling of not knowing what to do
° **nascent:** beginning

° **watered down:**
weakened (as if water
had been added to it)

for lack of a better term might be described as "broken"; my translation of
her Chinese, which could certainly be described as "watered down"° and
what I imagined to be her translation of her Chinese if she could speak in
perfect English, her internal language... I wanted to capture what language ability tests can never reveal: her intent, her passion, her imagery,
the rhythms of her speech and the nature of her thoughts.

° **verdict:** judgement,
decision (in a legal
case)

Apart from what any critic had to say about my writing, I knew I had
succeeded where it counted when my mother finished reading my book
and gave me her verdict:° "So easy to read."

Getting More Ideas through Discussion

Now it is time to get more ideas about the topic of this project by talking to your
classmates. By discussing and sharing your thoughts, you can come up with
more ideas than you can by just working alone. And by talking about your
ideas, you can make them clearer in your own mind.

Remember to talk about each of the discussion questions as a group and
take notes on the discussion. If you do not understand what someone says, ask
for clarification. Use the space below each question for your notes.

Discussion Questions

1. Do you like to write (for example, stories, poems, or essays) in your native
language? Why or why not? Find out *how* each member of your group feels
about writing and *why* she or he feels that way.

NAME	LIKES/DISLIKES WRITING	WHY?
1.		
2.		
3.		
4.		

2.   Most people agree that writing is the most difficult language skill. Even for native speakers of the language, it is hard to write well. But why is writing difficult? Discuss this question as a group and list all the reasons you can think of.

_____

_____

_____

_____

_____

_____

_____

_____

_____

_____

3.   What could you do to become a better writer? As a group, think of all the things that you could do to improve your writing, and explain how each one could affect your writing.

_____

_____

_____

_____

_____

_____

_____

_____

ESSAY TOPICS FOR PROJECT 2

By now you should have many ideas on the subject of this project, so it's time to write. Choose one of the following essay topics about writing.

1.   Of all the language skills, writing is the most difficult to master. This is true even for native speakers. Discuss the reasons that you think writing is difficult. Then suggest how you could solve some of your writing problems and become a better writer.

2.   Describe your history as a writer—where you learned to write compositions, how you learned, what kinds of things you wrote, and how much and how often you wrote. Then discuss whether or not you think this method was successful in teaching you to write well.

PREWRITING

Before you start your essay, explore and gather your thoughts. The brainstorming, reading, and discussion from earlier in the project are good sources of ideas.

Brainstorming

Brainstorm for ten minutes on your chosen topic. Use a separate sheet of paper for your brainstorming. This is part of your project and you will hand it in later. You can list or free-write, whichever you prefer. Just remember to write down everything that comes to mind. Don't stop to think about whether or not an idea is important or "correct."

Outlining

Some writers, especially academic writers, find it helpful to make an *outline* before they write. An outline is a list of the general and specific ideas that will be covered in the essay. The ideas are listed in the order they will be discussed. The outline serves as a guide to help the writer remember what he or she wants to say and organize the ideas before starting to write.

Look at the following for an example of an outline that I made for Topic 2.

MAIN IDEA : The way I was taught to write was not very successful.

A. My history of learning to write : how, where & what I wrote.
   1. writing in school
      a. elementary school
         wrote lots of stories, no poems, maybe reports
         teacher just corrected spelling
         put everyone's writing on wall
         everyone was "good" writer

      b. jr. & sr. high school
         much more writing — how often ?
         but no more stories, instead compositions/essays, reports, letters
         teacher showed grammar & spelling mistakes
         now not everyone was "good" writer anymore
         teachers gave grades, but no explanations, no comments or suggestions

      c. university
         assumed students already knew how to write
         no special courses — just freshman English
         students sink or swim

   2. writing outside school
      letters to friends, etc.
      diary sometimes — never for long time
      no stories or poems — not creative writer
      no help from parents — they didn't know either

B. This method was not successful because
   1. teachers only corrected - didn't comment or explain
      didn't show us examples of good essays

   2. students didn't read essays, mostly just textbooks

   3. students expected to learn by getting bad/good grade
      get bad grade — doing something "wrong"
      get good grade — doing something "right"

   4. more students didn't learn than did learn (even to be OK)
      those that learned acquired skill indirectly by selves
      I became OK writer, but not excellent

For this project, you are going to try outlining your essay before you write Draft One. The following instructions will guide you through the outlining process. Use a clean sheet of paper for your outline.

1.   At the top of the page write your main idea—the general idea you want your reader to remember, the idea that will unite your whole essay. You probably won't state it exactly the same way in your essay, but seeing it on paper in your outline will help you to clarify it in your mind. Check that your idea reflects what the assignment asks you to consider or discuss.

2.   Below your main idea write down each of your supporting ideas in the order you want to discuss them. Remember to leave space between points so you have room to develop them. Again, you may not state the supporting ideas exactly this way in your essay but seeing them on paper will help you to judge them. Check that each of your supporting ideas is relevant to your main idea.

After you've written your outline, brainstorm each supporting idea to come up with details and examples to develop it. Some writers brainstorm first and then outline. Some brainstorm and outline at the same time, especially when their time is limited. Some do not outline at all before they write. With practice, you can decide what works best for you.

However, if you choose to outline, remember that *an outline is only a guide.* It can be changed if you suddenly get another idea as you are writing. Since writing is a process of discovering what you want to say, you should not expect your final essay to always follow your outline exactly. But doing some organizing in advance can be helpful, especially when you don't have time to write more than one draft.

WRITING THE FIRST DRAFT

Now you are ready to write your first draft. Keep referring to your outline as you write. Using it as a guide, restate your ideas as full sentences and fill in more information or examples where necessary. Don't worry about minor grammatical errors or spelling. Don't worry about what your essay looks like as long as it is readable. Concentrate on developing the ideas in your outline as clearly and fully as you can. If you run out of ideas at any point, brainstorm again. Remember to double-space and write on one side of the page only.

When you have finished, read your essay from beginning to end. If possible, read it aloud. Hearing your words helps you to see your writing as a reader would see it. Continue to work on your essay until you are told to stop.

Finally, clip together your brainstorming, your outline, and your draft, and hand them all in to your teacher.

BEFORE STARTING READER RESPONSE AND REVISION, TURN
TO THE WRITING SKILLS SECTION BEGINNING ON PAGE 73.

READER RESPONSE

Writing is a lonely job. When you write, it's just you, a sheet of paper, and a pen, or you and a computer screen and keyboard. You become so involved with your piece of writing that it's difficult to stand "outside" it and see it objectively. For this reason, it's helpful to get another person's opinion. But getting feedback after you have finished the essay is really too late. Getting a response while you're still writing is more helpful.

So it is time to change hats—and papers—again and become a reader. Remember, your goal is not to look for grammatical or spelling mistakes (you will do that later) but to give your views as a reader about how successfully the writer has communicated ideas. This will help the writer to improve his or her writing, and it will also help you learn to look at your own writing from a reader's viewpoint.

> In this second project, you are going to focus on how fully the writer developed his or her ideas.

Don't be afraid to tell the writer if you think his or her ideas are not developed sufficiently. Many inexperienced writers do not give enough support to convince their readers. In fact, insufficient development is one of the most common weaknesses of student writing. Also don't be fooled by the number of words. Look at what the writer is saying, not how many words he or she uses to say it. Telling the writer in a constructive way what you think is not insulting; it is a way to help the writer make the next draft better.

Reader Response Sheet 2

Draft written by _____

Draft read by _____

Read the entire essay. If you can't understand any part, underline it and put a question mark next to it.

Questions to Answer

1. What do you think the writer's purpose is in this essay? (Look back at pages 11–12 if you have forgotten what *purpose* is.) _____

2. What is the writer's main idea? If it is directly stated, underline it and write it here. If there is no statement of the main idea, tell the writer. _____

_____

Is the main idea clearly stated? Do you fully understand it? _____

3. Does the writer's purpose and main idea answer the assignment?

Yes _____ Partly _____ No _____ (If no, give the essay back to the writer.)

Development of Ideas

1. Underline the topic sentence of each body paragraph and copy it below. If there is no topic sentence, write a sentence that you think expresses the point of the paragraph. If the paragraph is not unified (has no single idea clearly uniting the sentences), tell the writer.

_____

_____

_____

_____

_____

2. Has the writer given enough supporting ideas to convince you of the main idea?_____

3. Now look at the development of each body paragraph. Does the paragraph have enough details or explanation to support its topic sentence? Which paragraphs need more or better development? _____

Suggestions for Draft Two

What information could the writer add to strengthen each body paragraph?

_____

_____

_____

_____

_____

Essay Form

1. Is the essay appropriately divided into paragraphs? _____

2. Is each paragraph indented? _____

3. Is there an introduction and conclusion? _____

When you finish, return this response sheet and the draft to the writer.

Example of a Student Essay

To give you an example of a first draft and a reader's response to that draft, here is Draft One of the essay that a student, Su-Wung Yu, wrote about Topic One. It is followed by the Reader Response Sheet that a classmate filled out for Su-Wung.

[1]Many people think that writing is difficult. The first reason is you don't have enough information. So you have nothing about to write.

[2]The second reason, it is difficult to join and to put the ideas in right order when you are writing. Sometimes you don't know from which idea to start.

[3]However, there are several methods for good essay. First of all, think about your whole experience in your life.

[4]Another method for making your essay good is to copy works of the famous writers and to analyze their paragraphs. For example I can compare writing an essay and making a music composition. They have a common point. Frequently I copy a very famous musician's work several times because it shows me the motif and development. When you try this method in writing, you see the main idea and its development.

[5]Also teach somebody even if you are not good writer because when you teach someone, you can find what your problems are in your essay.

[6]Lastly, don't hesitate to rewrite and edit your essay several times. Don't forget your main idea. Often you escape from main idea when you write an essay.

Example of a Reader Response

The following Reader Response Sheet shows how a reader responded to Su-Wung's essay.

Questions to Answer

1. What do you think the writer's purpose is in this essay? (Look back at pages 11–12 if you have forgotten what *purpose* is.) *To explain why writing is difficult.*

2. What is the writer's main idea? If it is directly stated, underline it and write it here. If there is no statement of the main idea, tell the writer. _____

   Many people think that writing is difficult. _____

   Is the main idea clearly stated? Do you fully understand it? *Yes* _____

3. Does the writer's purpose and main idea answer the assignment?

   Yes *✓*___   Partly _____   No _____   (If no, give the essay back to the writer.)

Development of Ideas

1. Underline the topic sentence of each body paragraph and copy it below. If there is no topic sentence, write a sentence that you think expresses the point of the paragraph. If the paragraph is not unified (has no single idea clearly uniting the sentences), tell the writer.

   Writing is difficult because you don't have enough information. _____
   It is hard to put ideas in right order. _____
   A method for good essay is think about your whole experience in your life. ____
   Another method for making your essay good is to copy works of famous writers. _
   Teach somebody even if you are not good writer. _____
   Rewrite and edit your essay several times. _____

2. Has the writer given enough supporting ideas to convince you of the main idea? *Yes*

3. Now look at the development of each body paragraph. Does the paragraph have enough details or explanation to support its topic sentence? Which paragraphs need more or better development? *#1, 2 & 3* _____

Suggestions for Draft Two

What information could the writer add to strengthen each body paragraph?

In para. 1, separate introduction & list first reason & tell us what is result if you don't have ideas about what to write.

In para. 2, explain more why it is difficult to put ideas in right order.

In para. 3, explain how "think about whole experience in your life" is method for good essay. I don't understand how my experience makes better my writing.

Essay Form

1. Is the essay appropriately divided into paragraphs? *No (para. 1)*

2. Is each paragraph indented? *Yes*

3. Is there an introduction and conclusion? *No (no conclusion)*

When you finish, return this response sheet and the draft to the writer.

REVISING YOUR DRAFT

The next step in the project is to *revise* your essay. You will recall that revising is not just correcting your grammar and spelling, changing a few words, or re-copying Draft One more neatly. To revise means to re-see, to look at what you have written and then to change and improve it. But you must look at what is actually on the page—not at what you hope is there or wish were there!

There are many ways to revise your draft:

- You can add ideas (in the form of words, sentences, or whole paragraphs).
- You can combine ideas (by connecting sentences or paragraphs).
- You can eliminate ideas (words, sentences, or paragraphs).
- You can rephrase ideas (use different words to express ideas).
- You can shift the order of your ideas (by changing the position of words, sentences, or paragraphs).

Revision Questions

As you start Draft Two, think again about the goals you worked on in the previous project. Ask yourself the following questions.

- Do I have a clear main idea? Have I stated it at or near the beginning of the essay?
- Is my essay unified? Are all my supporting ideas relevant to my main idea?
- Is each paragraph unified? Are all the details in the paragraph closely related to the main idea of the paragraph?
- Did I write in essay form with an introduction, a body, and a conclusion?

In this second project you have an additional goal: to improve the development of your ideas. Think about your reader's comments and ask yourself these questions.

1. *Do I need more supporting ideas to develop my main idea? Or do I have too many different supporting points?*

   It's better to develop a few good ideas well than to develop many points superficially.

2. *Which supporting ideas need more or better development?*

   Remember what Amy Tan said about picturing a reader for her book and writing for that reader. Do the same. Think about who will read your essay and what that person needs to know in order to fully understand your ideas.

WRITING DRAFT TWO

If you are really unhappy with your first draft, or if you wrote off the topic, start all over again. More likely, however, you have some ideas you want to keep, so work with Draft One. As you did in the previous project, use Draft One as your base and make changes directly on your draft. This method of revising helps you to see what you have changed and what you have kept. Figure 2–1 shows part of the revision that Su-Wung Yu did for this project. Note that he worked directly on his draft.

Another method for making your ~~essay good~~ [writing better] is to [examine good writing]. copy works of the famous writers and ~~to~~ analyze their paragraphs. ~~For example I can~~ [This is what musicians] do to learn music composition. For example, Tchaikovsky frequently used to copy famous ~~compare writing an essay and making a music composition. They have a~~ musicians' work when he was studying about orchestral form. I do this too in my music studies. ~~common point.~~ Frequently I copy a very famous musician's work several

times because it shows me the motif and development. When you try this

method in writing, you see the main idea and [how is] it[s] develop[ed]~~ment~~.

Also teach somebody [to write] even if you are not good writer[,] ~~because~~ [yourself.] when you

teach someone, you can [discover what you don't know and] find what your problems are in your ~~essay.~~ [writing] ⊙

FIGURE 2–1   Example of revising

To check that you are really revising, make a list of your revisions, as you did for Project 1, and attach it to your draft. When you think you have finished, reread what you have written, from beginning to end. If possible, read your essay aloud. Listening to the sound of your writing helps you put yourself in your readers' shoes, and it can also help you discover missing words or careless errors.

Keep working on your essay for as long as time allows. As the writer Donald Murray notes:

> A piece of writing is never finished. It is delivered to a deadline, torn out of a typewriter on demand, sent off with a sense of accomplishment and shame and pride and frustration. If only there were a couple more days, time for just another run at it, perhaps then . . .

If your essay is still readable at this point, put it aside until it is time to edit. However, if you are a messy revisor or you have made so many revisions that your draft is illegible, make a clean copy. Remember to double-space and write on one side of the page only.

Example of a Student Revision

Here is the complete revised version (Draft Two) of Su-Wung Yu's essay about Topic One. Compare it to his first draft on page 63 to see what changes he made.

[1]Most people, even native speakers think that writing is a difficult skill to master. What makes writing hard? I think there are two reasons: getting information and organizing your ideas.

[2]The first reason is you must have enough information in order to write a good essay. If you don't have any thoughts about what to write, you will find it very difficult to support your ideas. You will stop writing after two or three lines because you don't have anything to say about the topic.

[3]The second reason is even if you have much information, you have to know how to organize your essay. Writing is different from speaking. When you speak you can say anything you like. You can jump from one topic to another topic if you want. However, you cannot do this way when you are writing. You must put the ideas in right order and join them properly or readers will not understand.

[4]However, there are several methods for improving your writing. First of all, read works by different writers—as many as possible. Also when you brainstorm think about all your experiences in your life that you could use as an example. Reading a lot and having many experiences will give you many ideas to write about.

[5]Another method for making your writing better is to examine good writing. Copy works of the famous writers and analyze their paragraphs. This is what musicians do to learn music composition. For example, Tchaikovsky frequently used to copy famous musicians' work when he was studying about orchestral form. I do this too in my music studies. Frequently I copy a very famous musician's work several times because it shows me the motif and development. When you try this method in writing, you see the main idea and how it is developed.

[6]Also teach somebody to write even if you are not good writer yourself. When you teach someone, you can discover what you don't know and find what your problems are in your writing.

[7]Lastly, don't hesitate to rewrite and edit your essay several times. If you are lazy to rewrite, you cannot improve your ideas, and if you are lazy to correct your grammar mistakes, people will not understand you.

[8]If you follow these methods, you can become a better writer.

After Su-Wung finished, he made a list of his revisions.

1. I wrote introduction and conclusion. So now I have correct essay form.
2. I wrote new topic sentence for two first body paragraphs and gave more information to support my ideas.

3. I put more information in paragraph 4 (old para. 3) to explain my idea.

4. I rewrote paragraph 5 (old para. 4). I wrote a new first sentence to tell the main idea of the paragraph. I made a better connection between writing and music, and I put in a specific example about a famous musician.

5. I added some details to paragraph 6 to make my idea more clear.

6. I took away part of old paragraph 6 (new para. 7), so now the paragraph has only one idea. Also I added some details to develop more that idea.

BEFORE YOU START TO EDIT, TURN TO THE GRAMMAR SECTION ON PAGES 195–203.

EDITING

In the drafts that you have written so far, you have concentrated on the content of your essay. You have worked to make your ideas clearer and more convincing to your readers, but you probably haven't paid much attention to grammar.

Now it is time to look closely at your grammar. It is time to edit your draft. Use Editing Checklist 2 on page 71 as a guide. Remember to use a different color pen or pencil when you edit so you can see the changes you make.

Steps in Editing

1. Read your paper carefully, looking for the kinds of problems listed on the Editing Checklist. Because you will read for only one type of error at a time, you will have to read your essay several times. Each time you finish reading for one kind of error, place a check next to it on the list.

2. Exchange papers with a partner and edit your partner's essay the same way you did your own. Looking at another student's paper can help you learn to spot your own grammatical errors.

> Editing may seem boring and you may want to rush through it, but it is one of the most important steps in writing. To find and correct your errors, you must train yourself to work patiently and thoroughly.

When you finish editing, hand in all the parts of your essay project to your teacher to check your revisions and corrections. When your essay is returned to you, remember to file it in your writing folder.

Editing Checklist 2

Draft checked by _____

Read your own essay carefully several times, each time looking for and correcting one kind of error on the list below. As you finish checking for each type of error, place a check (✔) next to it on the list.

When you finish editing your own essay, exchange papers with a classmate and edit each other's work.

_____ 1.   Basic sentence components

Missing or repeated subject

Missing verb

Missing or repeated object / complement

_____ 2.   Verbs

Wrong verb tense

Wrong verb form

_____ 3.   Agreement

No subject-verb agreement

_____ 4.   Sentence boundaries

Fragments

_____ 5.   Spelling (*Hint*: To check spelling, read each line of words from right to left. This will help you see each word individually.)

Teacher's comments: _____

_____

_____

_____

_____

When you finish editing, attach this sheet to your draft.

WRITING SKILLS: DEVELOPING YOUR IDEAS

Every language has its own rules about how to develop an idea, and English is no exception. In a written English passage, not all the ideas are of equal importance. English writers usually follow a pattern of making a general statement (the main idea) and then supporting it—explaining, describing, or illustrating it—with more specific information (the supporting ideas).

Usually the general statement comes first, but not always. Sometimes the more specific, supporting details are discussed first and are followed by the main idea. But in either case, the principle is the same.

> English readers expect general statements to be supported by specific details.

This expectation that English readers have about general and specific ideas does not apply to all languages. In some languages, writers provide mostly general statements and the reader accepts or rejects them based on his own specific knowledge or his faith in the writer. Students trained in this writing pattern, therefore, think that writing well means writing mostly general or abstract statements. They think that giving a lot of small details to explain specifically what they mean makes their writing sound childish or unimportant.

In other languages, writers are taught to provide mostly specific details and to leave the reader to draw his own conclusions or generalizations. Students who have learned to write this way think that mature readers should be able to make generalizations and to do so for them is to treat them like children.

> Writers of English—especially academic writers—are expected to include both general and specific information: to make general statements and to give specific details that show that the statements are true. If the writer gives only or mostly general statements without supporting details, we are unlikely to accept or believe the statements. And if the writer gives only specific details leaving the reader to make generalizations, we say the writer has not done a complete job.

This pattern of presenting general and specific ideas sounds easy to follow, but student writers often have problems because they are not sure of the difference between *general* and *specific*.

Differentiating between General Ideas and Specific Details

Let's look at an idea: "The city was incredibly dirty." Is this idea general or specific? Can you tell from the topic? No. Can you tell from the complexity of the idea? No. Can you tell from the words the writer chose? No. In fact, there is no way that you can answer this question.

Now look at the paired statements that follow. For each pair, which statement is more general (more inclusive) and which is more specific? Put a *G* next to the general statement and an *S* next to the specific statement.

A	**B**
1. New York City was an unpleasant place to live.	The city was incredibly dirty.
2. Pages of discarded newspapers littered the sidewalks.	The city was incredibly dirty.
3. Many sounds can be spelled several different ways.	The English spelling system is illogical.
4. Many sounds can be spelled several different ways.	The long *e* sound can be written *ee, ea,* or *ie.*
5. Although girls are not the only ones who dislike math, girls tend to drop math courses sooner than boys.	A 1972 survey of the amount of math taken by incoming freshmen at the University of California found that 57 percent of the boys had taken four years of high-school math while only 8 percent of the girls had.

Could you tell the difference between the general and the specific statements? If so, why could you in these cases but not in the first case?

Read the following passage from a book about writing by William Zinsser. In this paragraph from a chapter entitled "Simplicity," the author argues that a reader falls asleep or gets lost not because the reader is dumb or lazy but because the writer has been careless. Here Zinsser describes what he means by *carelessness*.

° **cluttered:** filled with unnecessary words
° **hacking:** cutting (plants in a jungle)
° **verbiage:** words
° **shoddily:** poorly, carelessly
° **switched:** changed
° **link:** connection
° **sanguine:** cheerful, optimistic
° **sanguinary:** bloody
° **bloody:** (slang) very
° **infer:** conclude, deduce
° **imply:** suggest

¹The carelessness can take any number of forms. ²Perhaps a sentence is so excessively cluttered° that the reader, hacking° through the verbiage,° simply doesn't know what it means. ³Perhaps a sentence has been so shoddily° constructed that the reader could read it in any of several ways. ⁴Perhaps the writer has switched° pronouns in mid-sentence, or has switched tenses, so the reader loses track of who is talking or when the action took place. ⁵Perhaps Sentence B is not a logical sequel to Sentence A—the writer, in whose head the connection is clear, hasn't bothered to provide the missing link.° ⁶Perhaps the writer has used an important word incorrectly by not taking the trouble to look it up. ⁷He may think that "sanguine"° and "sanguinary"° mean the same thing, but the difference is a bloody° big one. ⁸The reader can only infer° . . . what the writer is trying to imply.°

Look at each sentence in Zinsser's passage and decide whether it is more general, more specific, or the same compared to the sentences before and after it. The first sentence has been done for you.

more general ◄—————————► more specific

sentence 1.	_____✗_____	_____	_____
sentence 2.	_____	_____	_____
sentence 3.	_____	_____	_____
sentence 4.	_____	_____	_____
sentence 5.	_____	_____	_____
sentence 6.	_____	_____	_____
sentence 7.	_____	_____	_____
sentence 8.	_____	_____	_____

Notice how the writer moved from a general idea to more specific ideas, to even more specific ideas, and then back again toward a general idea.

Why, again, could you tell the difference between general and specific statements? The answer, of course, is because no idea can be a general idea all by itself, and no idea is specific or supporting all by itself. When we say an idea is *general* or *specific, main* or *supporting*, we refer not to the idea itself but to the relationship between the ideas. *Main* idea and *supporting* idea are relative terms; that is, *an idea is main or supporting only in relation to other ideas.* An idea that serves as a main idea in one essay or paragraph may be a supporting idea in another, and vice versa.

For example, look at the two paragraphs that follow. Both include the idea of making writing more interesting. But in one paragraph, the idea is used specifically, and in the other it is used generally. Can you tell which is which?

1. There are many devices that writers can use to make their writing interesting. One technique is to choose interesting examples that readers can identify with based on their own experience. Another way is to create images for the reader, to pull the reader into the writing by drawing pictures with words so the reader can "see" what the writer means. A third device is to use interesting vocabulary. Being able to choose just the right word, the word that is most appropriate or most meaningful in the context, is a skill all good writers have developed. Of course, none of these techniques can be learned overnight. They require a great deal of time and effort to acquire. But if you remember these hints and practice them, you too can make your writing more interesting.

2. Many students complain that writing is a difficult skill to learn. Why is that so? The answers are variable, but at least three reasons crop up repeatedly. It is hard, say inexperienced writers, to organize ideas logically. "I know what I want to say, but it just doesn't come out right on paper" is a common refrain. Another area of difficulty is making the writing interesting to the reader. All too often, students' writing is pedestrian. It has no spark, no energy. True, many of the topics that students are given to write about are dull, but even when the assignment is interesting, say students, it is difficult to write imaginatively. Finally, a third reason given is the diffi-

culty of choosing appropriate and varied vocabulary. Many students have never developed an extensive vocabulary, so when asked to write they have only a limited stock of words readily available. All of these difficulties can be overcome with hard work and perseverance. But students must be willing to put in the time and effort.

Remember, it is *how you use an idea* that makes it general or specific, not the idea itself.

Using Supporting Details

Often inexperienced writers complain they cannot think of any way to support a general idea. They don't know what kind of specific information might be appropriate. In fact, there are many ways to develop an idea. Good writers use: description, narration, logical reasoning, facts, statistics, quotations, personal experience, and illustrations or examples to support their ideas.

Let's look at three examples of how good writers develop their ideas. The paragraph that follows was written by Eudora Welty. It is taken from her autobiography *One Writer's Beginnings* in which she describes what influenced her to become a writer.

° **cadence;** rhythm in sound, the rise and fall of the voice in speaking
° **resides:** lives

> Ever since I was first read to, then started reading to myself, there has never been a line read that I didn't hear. As my eyes followed the sentence, a voice was saying it silently to me. It isn't my mother's voice, or the voice of any person I can identify, certainly not my own. It is human, but inward, and it is inwardly that I listen to it. It is to me the voice of the story or the poem itself. The cadence,° whatever it is that asks you to believe, the feeling that resides° in the printed word, reaches me through the reader-voice. I have supposed, but never found out, that this is the case with all readers—to read as listeners—and with all writers, to write as listeners. It may be part of the desire to write. The sound of what falls on the page begins the process of testing it for truth, for me. Whether I am right to trust so far I don't know. By now I don't know whether I could do either one, reading or writing, without the other.

1. What is the main idea of the paragraph? _____
   _____

2. How does Welty support that idea? _____

The next passage is about being a writer. It is the first part of an essay called "Talking about Writing" by Ursula Le Guin.

> ¹People come up to you if you're a writer, and they say, I want to be a writer. How do I become a writer?
>
> ² I have a two-stage answer to that. The first-stage answer is this: You learn to type (or to word-process). The only alternative is to have an inherited income and hire a full-time stenographer.° If this seems unlikely, don't worry. Keyboards are easy to learn.
>
> ³Well, the person who asked, How do I become a writer, is a bit cross° now, and mumbles, but that isn't what I meant. (And I say, I know it

° **stenographer:** person who can write rapidly in a special shorter form (shorthand)
° **cross:** angry

wasn't.) I want to write short stories, what are the rules for writing short stories? I want to write a novel, what are the rules for writing novels?

⁴Now I say Ah! and get really enthusiastic. You can find all the rules of writing in the book called *Elements of Style*, by Strunk and White, and a good dictionary—I recommend the *Shorter Oxford*; Webster's is too wishy-washy.° There are only a very few rules of writing not covered in those two volumes, and I can summarize them thus: Your story may begin in longhand° on the backs of old shopping lists, but when it goes to an editor, it should be typed, double-spaced, on one side of the paper only, with generous margins—especially the left-hand one—and not too many really grotty° corrections per page.

⁵Your name and its name and the page number should be on the top of every single page; and when you mail it to the editor it should have enclosed with it a stamped, self-addressed envelope. And those are the Basic Rules of Writing.

⁶I'm not being funny. Those are the basic requirements for a readable, therefore publishable manuscript.° And, beyond grammar and spelling, they are the only rules of writing I know.

⁷All right, that is stage one of my answer. If the person listens to all that without hitting me, and still says All right all right, but how *do* you become a writer, then I can deliver stage two. How do you become a writer? Answer: You write.

° **wishy-washy:** indecisive, having no set opinion

° **longhand:** ordinary writing by hand (not shorthand or typing)

° **grotty:** messy, dirty, disgusting (British slang)

° **manuscript:** draft of a book or article

1. What is the main idea of this passage? _____

    _____

2. How does the writer support this idea? _____

Finally, examine this last passage, about writing and rewriting. It is taken from an article called "The Maker's Eye: Revising Your Own Manuscripts" by Donald M. Murray.

¹When students complete a first draft, they consider the job of writing done—and their teachers too often agree. When professional writers complete a first draft, they usually feel that they are at the start of the writing process. When a draft is completed, the job of writing can begin.

²That difference in attitude is the difference between amateur and professional, inexperience and experience, journeyman° and craftsman.° Peter F. Drucker, the prolific° business writer, calls his first draft "the zero draft"—after that he can start counting. Most writers share the feeling that the first draft, and all of those which follow, are opportunities to discover what they have to say and how best they can say it. . . .

³Writers must learn to be their own best enemy. They must accept the criticism of others and be suspicious of it; they must accept the praise of others and be even more suspicious of it. Writers cannot depend on others. They must detach° themselves from their own pages so that they can apply both their caring and their craft° to their own work.

⁴Such detachment is not easy. Science fiction writer Ray Bradbury supposedly puts each manuscript away for a year to the day and then rereads it as a stranger. Not many writers have the discipline or the time to do this. We must read when our judgment may be at its worst, when we are close to the euphoric° moment of creation. . . .

⁵Most people think that the principal problem is that writers are too proud of what they have written. Actually, a greater problem for most pro-

° **journeyman:** worker who is still learning the job

° **craftsman:** skilled worker

° **prolific:** someone or something that produces a lot

° **detach:** separate (opposite of attach)

° **craft:** skill

° **euphoric:** exciting

fessional writers is one shared by the majority of students. They are overly critical, think everything is dreadful, tear up page after page, never complete a draft, see the task as hopeless.

° **prune:** to cut off a part to improve the form or shape (for example, of a tree)

[6]The writer must learn to read critically but constructively, to cut what is bad, to reveal what is good. Eleanor Estes, the children's book author, explains: "The writer must survey his work critically, coolly, as though he were a stranger to it. He must be willing to prune,° expertly and hardheartedly. At the end of each revision, a manuscript may look . . . worked over, torn apart, pinned together, added to, deleted from, words changed and words changed back. . . ."

° **spontaneous:** natural, unplanned

[7]Most readers underestimate the amount of rewriting it usually takes to produce spontaneous° reading. This is a great disadvantage to the student writer, who sees only a finished product and never watches the craftsman who takes the necessary step back, studies the work carefully, returns to the task, steps back, returns, steps back, again and again. Anthony Burgess, one of the most prolific writers in the English-speaking world, admits, "I might revise a page twenty times." Roald Dahl, the popular children's writer states, "By the time I'm nearing the end of a story, the first

° **altered:** changed

part will have been reread and altered° and corrected at least 150 times . . . Good writing is essentially rewriting. I am positive of this."

° **virtuous:** morally right or good

[8]Rewriting isn't virtuous.° It isn't something that ought to be done. It is simply something that most writers find they have to do to discover what they have to say and how to say it. It is a condition of the writer's life.

1. What do you think is the main idea of this passage? Write it here. _____

_____

2. Look at the kind of support the author uses. Look especially at paragraphs 2, 6, and 7. What kind of support does he use in these paragraphs? _____

_____

3. Look, too, at paragraph 3. How does he develop the central idea of this paragraph? _____

Finally, look back at Amy Tan's essay "Mother Tongue" at the beginning of this project. What is Tan's main idea? What kind of supporting information does she use in each paragraph?

Practice Using Supporting Details

Now it is time for you to try using different kinds of support in your writing. Two statements follow that are each the topic sentence of a paragraph. Write the rest of the paragraph. The instructions that precede each sentence suggest what form of support to use.

1. First try using *historical facts* to support the topic sentence. *Historical facts* are events that have actually happened or are known to be or accepted as being true.

History teaches us that no nation remains powerful forever.

_____

_____

_____

_____

_____

_____

_____

_____

2.   Now try using a *personal experience* as support. A *personal experience* is a real incident that happened to you. It refers to something you actually did or saw.

We are never too old to be embarrassed.

_____

_____

_____

_____

_____

_____

_____

_____

Judging Supporting Details

In the following three paragraphs, the writers try to use historical facts to support their main idea. How successful are they? Read each paragraph and answer the questions that follow it.

1.   History teaches us that no nation remains powerful forever. For example, from ancient Rome to modern times, no nation could remain powerful. This is true; we can study about it from history. Today we use this knowledge to form political policies. Hopefully international relationships will be better in the future.

Does the writer use historical facts to support the main idea? _____

If so: Are all the facts valid? (Are they true?) _____
          Are all the facts relevant to the main idea? _____
          Does the writer give enough facts to convince you that the main idea is possibly true? _____

2.   History teaches us that no nation remains powerful forever. I can say this is true for several reasons. First of all, if a nation becomes powerful, it also becomes richer in economic life. While the nation is getting rich, people can live more easily. They possibly get bored with their lives and do not work hard. They do not study any more; they do not know how to save, and they become interested in violence, drugs, or alcohol because they do not need anything. Therefore, the nation loses power.

Does the writer use historical facts to support the main idea? _____

If so: Are all the facts valid? (Are they true?) _____
       Are all the facts relevant to the main idea? _____
       Does the writer give enough facts to convince you that the main idea is possibly true? _____

3.   History teaches us that no nation remains powerful forever. In ancient times, Egypt, Greece, Rome, and China each dominated a part of the world. The Ottoman Turks controlled large areas of Europe, Asia, and North Africa from the fourteenth to the nineteenth century. Spain dominated the Americas from the 1500s to the 1800s. Britain, too, had a great empire around the world for many centuries; and in modern times, the former Soviet Union controlled a large portion of Europe and northern Asia. At the height of their power, all these nations probably believed that they were the exception, that no other country could surpass them. However, all eventually lost their dominant position in the world.

Does the writer use historical facts to support the main idea? _____

If so: Are all the facts valid? (Are they true?) _____
       Are all the facts relevant to the main idea? _____
       Does the writer give enough facts to convince you that the main idea is possibly true? _____

In the following three paragraphs, the writers try to use one extended example from their own experience to support the idea that New York is one of the dirtiest cities in the world. How successful are they? Again, read each paragraph and answer the questions that follow it.

1.   New York is one of the dirtiest cities in the world. The homeless lie on the street corners. When you pass them, the smell is terrible. Garbage fills the city. You can easily see dirty papers and cans on the street when you walk. The subway stations smell. Many people don't have moral concepts, so they just do whatever they want to do and they don't care what other people feel about it. I would like to suggest that the government face this problem.

Does the writer describe dirty conditions he or she personally saw or experienced? _____

If so: Does the writer describe one extended example? _____
Does the writer give you enough information to "see" or "smell" the situation? _____

2. New York is one of the dirtiest cities in the world. Most of the time, there is garbage on the street corners. Yesterday when I was walking along Broadway in Manhattan, I saw people littering all over the place. Many people don't follow the rule; they throw paper on the ground or leave garbage that does not belong there.

Does the writer describe dirty conditions he or she personally saw or experienced? _____

If so: Does the writer describe one extended example? _____
Does the writer give you enough information to "see" or "smell" the situation? _____

3. New York is one of the dirtiest cities in the world. I realized this the first time I took the subway. The entrance stairs were covered with squashed paper cups, old cigarette butts, and discarded candy wrappers. Inside the station the situation was no better. The platform was littered with pages of old newspapers and abandoned soda cans, and the tracks were almost buried in soggy garbage. The rats were having a good time, but I was disgusted. Every time I use the subway it's the same.

Does the writer describe dirty conditions he or she personally saw or experienced? _____

If so: Does the writer describe one extended example? _____
Does the writer give you enough information to "see" or "smell" the situation? _____

How Much Support Is Necessary?

Student writers often make the mistake of not giving enough support for their general ideas. But how much support is enough? Unfortunately, there is no easy answer to this question. It is like asking how much garlic should be put in spaghetti sauce! As all cooks know, the amount of garlic that should be used depends on many factors: the cook's preference, the strength of the garlic, and the tastes of the eaters.

Determining how much support to use in a piece of writing also depends on many factors. First, it depends on the relevance of the supporting ideas you use. One appropriate example is certainly better than two examples that don't really fit. Similarly, two valid or convincing reasons are stronger than three weak reasons.

How much support you use also depends on how much you know. A few correctly stated facts are better than five inaccurate ones.

It depends, too, on who your readers are and how much knowledge they have of the subject. For example, if you write about how filthy New York City is, people who have never been there might require more details to picture the dirty conditions than New Yorkers would need.

Finally, it depends on the nature of the assignment. If you are asked to write an essay, you will be expected to give more supporting information than you would give if you are asked just to write a paragraph about the same idea. If the assignment is a five-page essay or a one-hour writing period, you will be expected to explore the idea in greater depth than you would in a two-page essay or a half-hour writing period.

As you gain more experience as a writer and learn to think about your readers' needs, you will be able to judge whether or not you have succeeded in giving your readers as much information as they require.

Improving the Development of Ideas in Your Writing

Look back at the writing you have done so far in this course. Find an essay in which some of your ideas do not have sufficient supporting information. Choose one paragraph and rewrite it. Add more supporting details so that the paragraph is better developed. Write as many drafts of the paragraph as you feel are necessary. When you have finished, clip the improved paragraph to the original essay.

SUGGESTED JOURNAL TOPICS

1. My Thoughts about Writing Class

2. Erasmus, a sixteenth-century European scholar said, "The desire to write grows with writing." Is that true for you?

3. Define *a good writer*.

4.

© 1993 Frank Cotham

How will you enlarge your vocabulary?

5. My Pen's Thoughts

6. What is writing? Repeat the phrase *Writing is* all down the page and complete it differently each time.

7. How I Feel When I Have to Write an Essay

8. Here is an excerpt from the essay "How to Write a Personal Letter" by Garrison Keillor. Keillor is an American author and the host of a popular radio program called "A Prairie Home Companion." He is especially well known for his dry humor.

> Sit for a few minutes with the blank sheet in front of you, and meditate on the person you will write to. Let your friend come to mind until you can almost see her or him in the room with you. Remember the last time you saw each other and how your friend looked and what you said and what perhaps was unsaid between you, and when your friend becomes real to you, start to write.
>
> Write the salutation—Dear . . . —and take a deep breath and plunge in. A simple declarative sentence will do, followed by another and another and another. Tell us what you're doing and tell it like you were talking to us. Don't think about grammar, don't think about . . . [literary] style, don't try to write dramatically, just give us your news. Where did you go, who did you see, what did they say, what do you think?
>
> If you don't know where to begin, start with the present moment: *I'm sitting at the kitchen table on a rainy Saturday morning. Everyone is gone and the house is quiet.* Let your simple description of the present moment lead to something else, let the letter drift gently along.
>
> . . . If it's hard work to slip off a letter to a friend, maybe you're trying too hard to be terrific. A letter is only a report to someone who already likes you for reasons other than your brilliance. Take it easy.
>
> Don't worry about form. It's not a term paper. When you come to the end of one episode, just start a new paragraph. You can go from a few lines about the sad state of rock-n-roll to the fight with your mother to your fond memories of Mexico . . . to the kitchen sink and what's in it. The more you write, the easier it gets . . .

Pick up a piece of paper and, following Garrison Keillor's instructions, write a letter to your friend.

9. A Chinese proverb says, "I hear and I forget. I see and I remember. I do and I learn." How does this apply to learning to write?

10. Who are your favorite authors in your native language? Why do you like their writing?

11. Robert Frost, a popular American poet (1874–1963), said: "No tears in the writer, no tears in the reader." Do you agree?

12. Write your first name, one letter per line, down the length of the page. (If your first name is very short, use your last name, too.) For each letter, write a sentence in which all the words (or as many as possible) begin with that sound. The sentences can be as serious or as silly as you want.

13. Nonwriters often wonder where professional writers get their ideas. William Burroughs, a well-known American author, advises people to ". . . keep your eyes open. Notice what's going on around you." What's going on around *you*?

14. W. H. Auden, a British-American poet (1907–1973), said, "How can I know what I think till I see what I say?" Do you think that's true?

15.

" OPEN YOUR BOOKS TO PAGE 135. THERE ARE SOME THINGS THERE ENQUIRING MINDS OUGHT TO KNOW. "

© 1993 Frank Cotham

Imagine you are the author of the book. Write page 135.

16. Famous authors are often asked where they write best. Norman Mailer says, "I like a room with a view, preferably a long view. I dislike looking out on gardens. I prefer looking at the sea, or ships, or anything which has a vista to it." William Styron demands ". . . complete, noiseless privacy, without even music; a baby howling two blocks away will drive me nuts." Mary McCarthy wants "a nice peaceful place with some good light." And John Dos Passos says, "All you need is a room without any particular interruptions." Where do you prefer to write?

17. Look in an English dictionary and find five words you have never heard of, but whose sound intrigues you. What images or ideas do these words bring to your mind?

18. Pamela Margoshes, a humor and travel writer, has written a "Test for a Genuine Writer." The following five-question quiz is a shorter version of her original article. Read it and test yourself to see whether you are a "genuine" writer (scoring 9–15 points) or you flunk (scoring 6 points or less).

Give yourself three points for every "yes.". . .

***DO YOU ENJOY WATCHING OTHER PEOPLE'S VACATION SLIDES, EVEN IF THEY'RE BLACK AND WHITE AND FUZZY AROUND THE EDGES? Real writers look forward eagerly to four hours of watching fuzzy black-and-white pictures of other people's vacation trips.

Genuine writers understand that mystery, intrigue, and glamour can be found in even the simplest and most innocent seeming pictures. Real writers love the drama in other people's family slides. Their imaginations get all fired up by listening to other people describe their vacation.

***CAN YOU TELL A JOKE IN FRONT OF AN AUDIENCE?** Real writers cannot tell jokes successfully in front of more than one person. They may begin well enough. It's the endings they find difficult.

Writers are word lovers. They get caught in the syntax of a joke. They love the process of telling jokes more than getting to the actual punchlines.

Writers are so used to revising and revising and revising that they get stuck in the middle of a joke. They tend to return immediately to the beginning.

Or they'll think of a million ways to end the joke—and will try out all of them, one by one.

***DO YOU FIND YOURSELF IRRESISTIBLY ATTRACTED TO YOUR NEIGHBOR'S TRASH IN THE MIDDLE OF THE NIGHT?** Your neighbors, who are not at all famous, are fascinating to you. And so, at two in the morning, when you can't think of anything to write, you find yourself searching through their garbage in the big decorated plastic pails by their garage. You want to know everything about them. Spying on the neighbors will free you from writer's block.

***DO YOU LOOK FORWARD TO DISASTER AND CATASTROPHE?** Do you love it when terrible things happen? Do you live your life hoping to sell your horror story to a famous tv program? Do you think of your life as a magazine article waiting to happen?

Do you think of personal misfortune as the best way to get material to write about without doing any research?

If this sounds like you—you're a real writer.

***DO YOU ALWAYS WEAR THE SAME GRUBBY CLOTHES WHILE WRITING?** Genuine writers understand the value of dressing down while they work. Can a real writer wear designer jeans and still be inspired? What about a writer who likes polyester? Maybe yes, maybe no—but why take the chance?

Writers are very suspicious about where their inspiration comes from. They think they are more likely to be inspired if they are casually, even poorly dressed.

So check your wardrobe now. If you've got anything even remotely fashionable in it—get rid of it immediately.

19. According to well-known author Gloria Steinem, "Writers are notorious for using any reason to keep from working: over-researching, retyping, going to meetings, waxing the floors—anything." What do you do when you have to write and you don't feel like it?

20.

THE FAR SIDE   By GARY LARSON

"Well, time for our weekly brain-stem-storming session."

Choose a topic (appropriate to dinosaurs) for them to brainstorm about, and write the dialogue. Be sure every dinosaur in the group participates.

ADDITIONAL WRITING TOPICS

1. Increasingly in American and Canadian universities, students (both native and non-native speakers) who have completed all their required English composition courses continue to be poor writers and cannot successfully complete the writing assignments in their subject courses. Write a letter to the editor of your school newspaper suggesting ways to help solve this problem.

2. Most American and Canadian universities require entering students to prove they have a minimal level of writing skills to take college level courses. Many of them do this by requiring all new students to write an essay on a given topic in a set time period. Discuss the advantages and disadvantages of using this kind of test to measure students' writing ability. Then suggest other possible ways students could be evaluated.

3. Speaking and writing are similar skills in the sense that both require the production of language. Yet most people say that even in their native language it is harder to write than to speak. What is the difference between speaking and writing? Which do you find more difficult and why?

4. Reread the essay by Amy Tan on pages 54–56. What factors does she say discouraged and encouraged her to become a writer? Did you ever consider becoming a writer in your native language? What encouraged or discouraged you?

ADDITIONAL READINGS

Margaret Atwood. "Great Unexpectations." *Ms Magazine*, July-August 1987. Reprinted in *Major Modern Essayists*, 2nd ed. Edited by Gilbert H. Muller and Alan F. Crooks. Englewood Cliffs, New Jersey: Prentice-Hall 1994.

John Kenneth Galbraith. "Writing and Typing." *Atlantic Monthly*. March 1978. Reprinted in *The Dolphin Reader*, pp. 1020–1027. Edited by Douglas Hunt. Boston: Houghton Mifflin 1986.

Donald M. Murray. "The Maker's Eye: Revising Your Own Manuscripts." *The Writer*. October 1973. Revised version reprinted in *Patterns of Exposition 10*, pp. 152–157. Edited by Randall E. Decker. Boston: Little, Brown and Company 1986.

Richard Rodriguez. "Mr. Secrets." *Hunger of Memory: The Education of Richard Rodriguez*. Chap. 6. Boston: David R. Godine 1982. Reprinted in *The Dolphin Reader*, pp. 989–1003. Edited by Douglas Hunt. Boston: Houghton Mifflin 1986.

William Stafford. "A Way of Writing." *Field*. Spring 1970. Reprinted in *The Riverside Reader*, 4th ed. Edited by Joseph F. Trimmer and Maxine Hairston. Boston: Houghton Mifflin 1993.

P R O J E C T
3
NEW LIVES

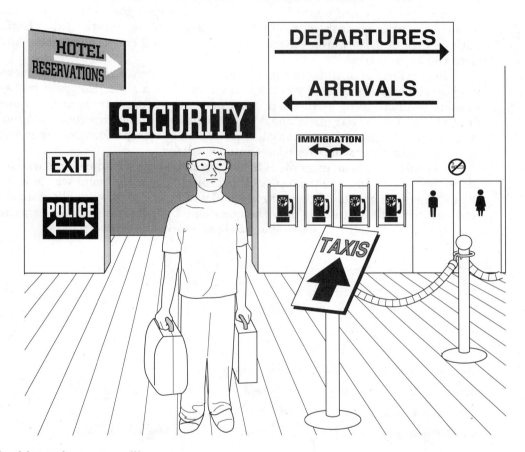

In this project, you will

- try another method for generating ideas and getting them down on paper before you write: asking wh– questions.

- think about the introduction to an essay and practice writing introductions.

- examine how English writers ensure that their readers can follow their ideas easily.

- practice improving the flow of ideas in your own writing.

- write several assignments about your experiences and thoughts about coming to a new country.

- continue to practice critical reading and revision.

- continue to practice editing your writing.

- continue writing in your journal.

GETTING IDEAS

You have practiced listing and free-writing as methods of getting ideas on paper. Now you will look at a third way to generate ideas and write them down so you can begin to use them in your writing.

Brainstorming Method 3: Asking Wh– Questions

Another brainstorming technique is to ask yourself as many questions as you can about the topic and answer them briefly. Since your goal is to get as many ideas as possible, you ask yourself wh– questions: that is, questions that begin with or include *wh–* words—*what, which, why, where, when, how, who.* And then you answer them.

In this form of brainstorming, you act as if you were a reporter interviewing yourself to find out what you know or think about a topic. However, just as in other brainstorming methods, it is not necessary to organize your questions or answers. Write your questions down in whatever order they come to mind. Also you do not have to write complete sentences or worry about grammar and spelling. Just write whatever comes into your head.

The following is an example of brainstorming using wh– questions which I did for an essay related to the topic of this project. The assignment was to write about "Something Old and Something New" and I decided to write about an old and new job. Here I include only the questions I generated. (When you write your questions, be sure to leave space to brainstorm the answers.)

What is my new job?
What was my old job?
How are old & new jobs alike/different?
Why change jobs?
Which job do I like better?
What was best/worst about old job?
What is good/bad so far about new job?
How long did I have the old job?
Which job has better pay? Benefits? Working conditions?
What is a job?
When did I change jobs?
How did I feel when started new job? When ended old job?
How easy/difficult to get new job?
How did it feel to go for job interviews?
Why have a job?

Now to start this project, you are going to ask wh– questions as a technique for generating and writing down your ideas.

STARTING TO THINK ABOUT THE TOPIC OF THIS PROJECT

For this project, you are going to write about your thoughts, feelings, and experiences as a newcomer to this country. To start, think back to when you first arrived here. Brainstorm for fifteen minutes on: "My First Days and Weeks Here." Use the space provided for your questions and answers.

_____

_____

_____

_____

_____

_____

_____

_____

_____

_____

_____

_____

_____

_____

_____

_____

_____

_____

_____

_____

Getting Ideas through Reading

1.   Have you ever been away from your native country before? Did you visit as a tourist or did you live in the new country? Is there a difference between being a tourist and living in a country for an extended period?

2.   While in this country, do you prefer spending your time with Americans or with people from your own country? Why? Is language the only difference between you and native English speakers?

3.   When people move to another country with a culture that is different from the one they grew up with, they often feel anxious and alienated. Social scientists call this feeling *culture shock*. Do you think it is possible to get over this feeling? Do you think you will ever feel as natural and comfortable here as you did in your own country?

Amparo Ojeda was born and raised in the Philippines. She came to the United States for the first time as a graduate student to study for an M.A. in linguistics. After completing her degree, she went back to the Philippines to continue her education, but several years later she returned to the United States to live permanently. She is now a professor at Loyola University of Chicago. In this excerpt from her essay "Growing Up American: Doing the Right Thing," she writes about her first impressions of Americans.

° **encounter:** meeting

° **gaze:** look, stare
° **romp:** play by running and jumping

° **ambivalence:** having opposite or conflicting feelings
° **fare:** get along

° **beaming:** smiling

° **Fulbright scholars:** participants in a U.S. government-sponsored educational exchange program that brings foreign students and faculty to study in the U.S. and sends Americans abroad.
° **briefing:** meeting in which information or instructions are given out before an activity
° **leg:** part
° **sojourn:** stay
° **theoretical survival kit:** suggestions on how to get along in another country
° **discrepancies:** differences
° **fidgeting:** moving about restlessly

The earliest . . . encounter° that I had with Americans . . . goes back to my childhood days when an American family moved into our neighborhood. I used to gaze° at the children, a boy and a girl, who were always neatly dressed and who would romp° around their fenced front yard. Not knowing their names, I, together with a cousin, used to call them "Hoy, Americano!" (Hey, American!), and they themselves soon learned to greet us with "Hey Filipino!" That was as far as our "acquaintance" went because in no time at all they were gone, and we never again heard about them.

That brief encounter aroused my curiosity. I wanted to know something more about the "Americanos." What kind of people are they? What food do they eat? Where is America? As time passed, I learned about America— about the people and about some aspects of their lifestyle—but my knowledge was indirect. The opportunity to experience the world of the "Americano" directly was long in coming, and when it did I was gripped with a sense of ambivalence.° How would I fare° in a strange and foreign land with an unfamiliar culture? That was how I finally found myself on the plane that would bring me . . . to Hawaii. . . .

My host family during my brief two-week stay in Honolulu was waiting at the airport. The whole family was there! The children's beaming° faces and the family's warm and gracious greetings gave me a sense of assurance that everything was going to be fine. "There's nothing to it," we Fulbright scholars° were reassured during a briefing° on aspects of adjustment to American life and culture. So there I was in Hawaii, the first leg° of my cultural sojourn.° [Next] I stayed in the Midwest for another four weeks of orientation, before proceeding east to do graduate work), equipped with a theoretical survival kit° designed and guaranteed to work. I would later discover that there were discrepancies° between the ideal procedures and techniques and day-to-day behavior.

The differences between my culture and American culture became evident in the first few hours after my arrival. On our way out of the air terminal, the children began to fuss: "I'm hungry," "I'm tired," "I'm thirsty," "I want to go to the bathroom!" Over the whining and fidgeting° of the children, my hosts and I tried to carry on a conversation but to no avail. Amazingly, despite the constant interruptions, the adults displayed considerable tolerance and patience. No voice was raised, nor harsh words spoken. I vividly recall how, as children, we were reminded never to interrupt while adults were talking, and to avoid annoying behavior, especially when in

° **kin:** relatives

the company of adults, whether these people were kin,° friends, or strangers.

We left the main highway, drove on a country road, and eventually parked by a Howard Johnson restaurant. The children did not need any bidding at all. They ran inside the restaurant in search of a table for us. I was fascinated by their quite independent and assertive behavior. . . . As soon as we were all seated, a young man came to hand us menus. The children made their own choices. Not feeling hungry at all, but wanting to show appreciation, I settled for° a cup of soup. When the food finally came, I was completely shocked by the portions each child had. I wondered if they could eat it all. Just as I feared, they left their portions only partially eaten. What a waste, I thought. I remembered one of my father's gems of thought: "Take only what you can eat, and make sure to eat the last morsel° on your plate." I must confess that I felt very bad looking at mounds of uneaten food. How can so much food be wasted? Why were children allowed to order their food themselves instead of Mom and Dad doing it for them? Was it a part of independence training? Or were Mom and Dad simply indulgent° of their children's wants? I did not have any answers, but I surmised° that it wasn't going to be easy understanding the American way. Neither would it be easy accepting or adjusting to American customs. I realized later that my difficulty was brought about by my cultural bias and naivete.° Given the situation, I expected my own familiar behavioral-cultural response. For instance, in the Philippines . . . children are rarely allowed, if at all, to "do their own thing" without the consent of their parents. Consultation° with parents, older siblings, aunts and uncles, or grandparents is always sought. In America, I found out that from an early age, a person is encouraged to be independent, to make up his or her mind, and to stand up for his or her rights. Individualism is encouraged among the American youth, whereas among . . . Filipinos, group unity, togetherness, and harmony are valued.

[In the Philippines] values such as obedience to authority . . . and respect for elders are seriously observed and practiced. The young address their elders using terms of respect. . . . Not to do so is considered rude. Children do not call anybody older by their first names. This deference° to age contrasts sharply with the American notions of egalitarianism° and informality.

American children, I observe, are allowed to call older people by their first names. I recall two interesting incidents, amusing now but definitely bothersome then. The first incident took place in the university cafeteria. To foster° collegiality° among the faculty and graduate students, professors and students usually ate lunch together. During one of these occasions, I heard a student greet a teacher, "Hey Bob! That was a tough exam! You really gave us a hard time, buddy!"° I was stunned. I couldn't believe what I heard. All I could say to myself was, "My God! How bold and disrespectful!"

Not long afterward, I found myself in a similar scenario.° This time, I was with some very young children of new acquaintances. They called to say hello and to ask if I could spend the weekend with the family. At their place, I met more people, young and not so young. Uninhibited,° the children took the liberty of° introducing me to everybody. Each child who played the role of "introducer" would address each person by his or her first name. No titles such as "Mr.," "Mrs.," or "Miss" were used; we were simply introduced as "Steve, this is Amparo" and "Amparo, this is Paula." Because I was not acquainted with . . . American communicative style, this

° **settled for:** accepted (without really wanting)

° **morsel:** tiny piece, mouthful

° **indulgent:** permissive, allowing someone to do or have what he wants
° **surmised:** inferred, guessed
° **naivete:** lack of experience in expected social rules or behavior
° **consultation:** a meeting to get advice or information

° **deference:** respect
° **egalitarianism:** idea that all people are equal and should have equal rights and opportunities

° **foster:** encourage
° **collegiality:** friendly relationships

° **buddy:** informal way to address a man (especially when you are upset or angry)
° **scenario:** situation

° **uninhibited:** without any restrictions on their feelings or actions
° **took the liberty of . . . :** did something without asking permission

° **muster:** gather, collect

took me quite by surprise. I was not prepared for the reality of being ad-dressed as the children's equal. In my own experience it took me some time to muster° courage before I could call my senior colleagues by their first names.

Getting More Ideas through Discussion

It is time to talk to your classmates and discover what ideas they have about the topic of this project. Talk about each of the discussion questions as a group and take notes on what each person says. You can use the space below each question for your notes. Remember:

1. Everyone must participate in the discussion. Questioning each other encourages everyone to explore his or her ideas and opinions.
2. Write down all the responses. You never know what ideas will be use-ful to you later.

Discussion Questions

1. Before you came to this country, what did you think life here was like? Where or from whom did you get this information?

NAME	MY IDEAS ABOUT THIS COUNTRY BEFORE I CAME HERE	SOURCE OF INFORMATION

2.   Now that you have lived in this country for several months or perhaps even several years, you probably have developed different opinions about it. Based on your experience of actually living here, how would you now describe life in this country?

NAME	MY IDEAS ABOUT THIS COUNTRY NOW

3.   Think about how *you* have changed since you came here. How is *your* behavior or way of thinking here different from that in your own country? When you have finished, share your answers with your group.

IN MY COUNTRY	HERE

ESSAY TOPICS FOR PROJECT 3

Now that you have gathered some ideas about the subject of this project, it is time to write. Choose one of the following essay topics about coming to live in a new country.

1.   Sometimes the real situation we find in a new country matches our preconceived ideas about that country, and sometimes it does not. Has this country turned out to be like you thought it would? Compare your preconceptions to the reality you found.

2.   Many people who come to live in this country become "Americanized." They adopt new ways of behaving and thinking. How have you changed since you came here? Compare your behavior and ideas here with the way you (or people your age) act and think in your country.

PREWRITING

The first step in writing your essay is to generate some ideas and get them on paper. The brainstorming, reading, and discussion from earlier in the project are good sources of ideas.

Brainstorming

Brainstorm for ten minutes on your chosen topic. Use a separate sheet of paper for your brainstorming. This is part of your project and you will hand it in later. You can list, free-write, or ask wh– questions, whichever you prefer. Just remember to write down everything that comes to mind. Don't stop to think about whether or not an idea is important or "correct."

Outlining

After you have brainstormed, decide whether or not you want to make an outline. If you found it helpful in Project 2 to choose and organize your ideas in outline form before starting to write, take time now and write an outline for your essay.

WRITING THE FIRST DRAFT

Now you are ready to write your first draft. If you made an outline, use it as a guide for your draft. If you only brainstormed, refer to your brainstorming notes as a source of ideas. Concentrate on choosing, organizing, and developing your ideas as clearly and fully as you can. Don't worry about minor grammatical errors or spelling. Don't worry about what your essay looks like as long as it is readable. If you run out of ideas at any point, brainstorm again. Double-space so you have room to revise later on, and write on one side of the page only.

When you have finished, read your essay from beginning to end. If you can, read it aloud and listen to your words. If any part doesn't sound "right," rethink it and rewrite it. Continue to work on your essay until the period is over. Then clip together all your prewriting, (your brainstorming plus your outline if you wrote one) and your draft, and hand them in to your teacher.

BEFORE STARTING THE READER RESPONSE AND REVISION SECTIONS, TURN TO THE WRITING SKILLS SECTION BEGINNING ON PAGE 109.

READER RESPONSE

Now it is time to change roles again and look at a classmate's paper. Remember, the purpose of your reading is not to correct grammatical mistakes but to give your views as a reader.

In this project, you are going to focus on the introduction to the essay and the organization of ideas in the essay.

Reader Response Sheet 3

Draft written by _____

Draft read by _____

Read the entire essay. If you can't understand any part, underline it and put a question mark next to it.

Questions to Answer

1. What do you think the writer's purpose is in this essay? _____

_____

2. What is the writer's main idea? If it is directly stated, underline it and write it here. If there is no statement of the main idea, tell the writer. _____

_____

Is the main idea clearly stated? Do you fully understand it? _____

3. Does the writer's purpose and main idea answer the assignment?

Yes _____   Partly _____   No _____   (If no, give the essay back to the writer.)

Introduction

1. Is there an introduction? _____

If yes, does it inform you of the topic? _____   Does it state the main idea? _____

Does it catch your attention? _____   If yes, how? _____

_____

2. Suggestions for improving the introduction: _____

_____

_____

Development and Organization of Ideas

1. How did the writer organize the ideas? Look at the patterns on pages 109–111.

Side-by-side _____   Point-by-point _____   Unclear _____

On a separate sheet of paper, outline the essay. If you can't easily find or state the supporting points, tell the writer in your Suggestions for Draft Two.

2.   Are there enough supporting ideas to convince you of the writer's point of view? _____

3.   For each supporting point, does the writer give information about both sides? _____

Which points are one-sided? _____

_____

_____

4.   Is each supporting point sufficiently developed so you really understand what the writer means?_____   Which need more development? _____

_____

_____

Suggestions for Draft Two

_____

_____

_____

_____

When you finish, return this response sheet and the draft to the writer.

Example of a Student Essay

The essay that follows is the first draft that a student, Michael Sung Hyun Lim, wrote in response to Topic One.

[1] I was in a restaurant with my close friends drinking bitter wine. They made toasts for my future, and they encouraged me to live well in the U.S. I'll never forget it. At that time, I thanked them, but on the other hand, my mind was very complicated. After getting home I couldn't sleep. I was worried about my future in the unknown world, and I thought a lot about my life in the new homeland.

[2] The direct motivation for my family to immigrate here is for my education. In my country, I couldn't go to college because I failed the exam to go to college. And I heard that it was easier to continue education in the U.S. than in my native country. In other words I thought there were more opportunity of education in the U.S. That is true. I know that simply. I am a college student now and I'll be able to go to graduate-college and even I'll be able to get Ph.D. if I want to and try to.

[3] In the airplane, on the way here, I thought. I could get more possibilities in the U.S. than I could get in my own country. Because the U.S. is a big country in its size as well as economically. And it is one of leading countries of the world. I don't know yet about this preconception because I'm not educated enough and I have only a few experiences. But I can feel this; if I try hard, I'll able to do anything.

[4] A few months ago, when I got here I was really worried about English. But my friends said, "If you live there, you will speak English well." That is wrong. I've been here for about ten months. But I don't speak English well. Because I didn't try hard. So, I can be aware of this proverb "Heaven helps those who help themselves."

[5] And I thought New York was very big and clean city. But as soon as I arrived at the airport, I was disappointed. A lot of garbage were here and there. And at the subway stations I just couldn't breathe because of bad smell.

[6] In conclusion, some of my conceptions turned out true, but some didn't. However, I believe that the U.S. is the land of opportunity so I'll try my best for my future.

Example of a Reader Response

The following Reader Response Sheet shows how a classmate responded to Michael's essay.

Questions to Answer

1. What do you think the writer's purpose is in this essay? *To compare your ideas about America before you came here and after you came here.*

2. What is the writer's main idea? If it is directly stated, underline it and write it here. If there is no statement of the main idea, tell the writer. *Some of my conceptions turned out true and some didn't.*

Is the main idea clearly stated? Do you fully understand it? *yes.*

3. Does the writer's purpose and main idea answer the assignment?

Yes _✓_ Partly _____ No _____ (If no, give the essay back to the writer.)

Introduction

1. Is there an introduction? *yes.*

If yes, does it inform you of the topic? *yes.* Does it state the main idea? *no.*

Does it catch your attention? *yes.* If yes, how? *You used a personal example about drinking with your friends. It was interesting.*

2. Suggestions for improving the introduction. *1) Maybe include a statement of main idea of the essay. 2) When did you go to this restaurant? 3) Why was wine bitter? Do you drink cheap wine?*

Development and Organization of Ideas

1. How did the writer organize the ideas? Look at the patterns on pages 109–111.

Side-by-side _____ Point-by-point _✓_ Unclear _____

On a separate sheet of paper, outline the essay. If you can't easily find or state the supporting points, tell the writer in your Suggestions for Draft Two.

2. Are there enough supporting ideas to convince you of the writer's point of view? *yes.*

3. For each supporting point, does the writer give information about both sides? *yes.*

Which points are one-sided? *All of them but especially #3.*

4. Is each supporting point sufficiently developed so you really understand what the writer means? *no* Which need more development? *point #2 about possibilities.*

Suggestions for Draft Two

1) Cross out point #4. It is not important like points 1–3.

2) Give more information about ideas before you came to America.

3) Explain what you mean by possibilities. I don't understand this.

4) I think proverb in paragraph 4 is not related.

REVISING YOUR DRAFT

Revision Questions

As you start Draft Two, think again about the goals you worked on in the previous projects. Ask yourself the following questions.

- Is my main idea really clear?
- Do I have enough support for my main idea to convince my readers?
- Are all my supporting ideas relevant?
- Is each supporting idea expressed clearly?
- Is each supporting idea sufficiently developed?

In this third project you have two additional goals: to improve the introduction to your essay and to improve the organization of your ideas. Look at your reader's comments and ask yourself these questions.

1. *Does my introduction inform the reader of the topic of my essay? Does it focus the reader's attention on my main idea? Is it interesting to read; does it capture the reader's attention?*

There are a number of ways to improve your introduction: write a whole new paragraph, keep your first effort but rephrase some of the sentences, add more information, or rearrange the order of the sentences.

2. *Have I clearly organized the body of my essay?*

To check your organization, look at your reader's outline of your essay. Does it clearly follow either the point-by-point or the side-by-side pattern? If not, choose the form you think will work better for your essay and make a new outline to use as a guide for writing Draft Two.

As you revise, or when you have finished revising, make a list of all the changes and attach it to your draft.

Then reread your whole draft. If possible, read aloud to yourself. Listening to the sound of your writing helps you hear it through different ears and can also help you discover careless errors.

Finally, if your draft is no longer readable, recopy it. Remember to double-space and write on one side of the page only.

Example of a Student Revision

Figure 3–1 shows how Michael Lim revised the first two paragraphs of his essay using Draft One as a base. Notice how he added or changed words, and eliminated, rewrote, or added whole sentences as he struggled to express his ideas better.

A year ago I was in a restaurant with my close friends drinking ~~bitter~~ wine.

They made toasts for my future, and they encouraged me to live well in the U.S. ~~I'll never forget it.~~ At that time, though I thanked them, ~~but on the other hand,~~ my mind was very ~~complicated~~ upset. After getting home I couldn't sleep for a long time.

I was worried about my future in the unknown world, ~~and~~ I thought a lot about my life in the new homeland. Now one year later some of those thoughts turned out true and some didn't.

The direct motivation for my family to immigrate here is for my education. In my country I couldn't go to college after graduating from high school because I failed the entrance exam. So I had to wait for a year preparing for that terrible test again. That circumstance made me and my parents decide to move here. Everybody told me that it would be ~~to go to college. And I heard that it was~~ easier to continue education in the U.S. than in my native country. That was my thought too, ~~In other words I thought there were more opportunity of education in the U.S.~~ That and it is true. I know that from my present status as simply I ~~am~~ a college student. ~~now and I'll be able to go to graduate-~~ I think I could get even more opportunities for my education if I try hard enough. ~~college and even I'll be able to get Ph.D. if I want to and try to.~~

FIGURE 3–1   Example of revising

Now look at the complete revised essay. In response to his reader's comments, Michael worked to improve his introduction and the organization and development of his ideas. Compare Draft Two with Draft One (page 101) to see what changes he made.

[1]A year ago I was in a restaurant with my close friends drinking wine. They made toasts for my future, and they encouraged me to live well in the U.S. At that time, though I thanked them, my mind was very upset. After getting home I couldn't sleep for a long time. I was worried about my future in the unknown world. I thought a lot about my life in the new homeland. Now one year later some of those thoughts turned out true and some didn't.

[2]The direct motivation for my family to immigrate here is for my education. In my country I couldn't go to college after graduating from high school because I failed the entrance exam. So I had to wait for a year preparing for that terrible test again. That circumstance made me and my parents decide to move here. Everybody told me that it would be easier to continue education in the U.S. than in my native country. That was my thought too, and it is true. I know that simply from my present status as a college student. I think I could get more opportunities for my education if I try hard enough.

[3]The U.S. is well-known as a country that is big and rich and that leads liberal democratic countries. So I thought that there would be more chances to succeed in life in the U.S. I can't judge whether that is true or not because I don't know America well and I have few experiences in this society. But I can feel the U.S. offers more possibilities. And these possibilities give me more reasons for trying harder.

[4]When I knew that I would emigrate to the U.S. I was really worried about English. But my friends said, "You'll learn English unconsciously because you'll live in a country where English is spoken." I hoped so. However, the result, after 10 months, is miserable. Sometimes I'm really frustrated because of my poor English. Although English is very essential, I admit not devote my effort to it. Now I can confirm that nothing has been done without effort and sweat. I need English not to become a "fish out of water."

[5]Now I am forming new ideas about my future which are different from the preconceptions that I made in my native country. I believe that the U.S. is the land of opportunity. I won't wait for what America will do for me, but I will find my own chances and will make my own life in this country.

After Michael finished, he made a list of his revisions.

1. In the introduction, I reworded some parts of sentences, and I added a sentence at the end about my main idea.

2. In paragraph 2, I added more information and rewrote some sentences.

3. I completely rewrote paragraph 3.

4. I also rewrote paragraph 4. I developed the idea more.

5. I took out paragraph 5 about New York as a big and clean city. (My reader said it wasn't important.)

6. I wrote a new conclusion. I tried to make it more interesting.

BEFORE STARTING TO EDIT, TURN TO THE GRAMMAR SECTION ON PAGES 204–209.

EDITING

It is again time for the last step in the writing process: correcting your grammar and spelling. That is, it is time to edit your essay. Use the Editing Checklist on page 107 as a guide, and remember to edit in a different color pen or pencil.

Steps in Editing

1. Read your own paper carefully, checking for the kinds of errors on the checklist.

2. Exchange papers with a partner, and read your partner's paper carefully, looking for the same kinds of errors.

> Don't worry that your paper is not grammatically perfect; you can't correct every error you make. But if you can learn to spot at least those errors outlined on the Editing Checklist, you can significantly improve the accuracy of your writing and the impression you make on your reader.

When you finish editing, hand in the whole project (your prewriting, all the drafts, the Reader Response Sheet, your revision list, and the Editing Checklist) to your teacher to check your changes and corrections. When your essay is returned to you, remember to file it with the rest of your writing assignments. Do not throw any writing away.

Editing Checklist 3

Draft checked by _____

Read your essay carefully several times, each time looking for and correcting one kind of error on the list below. As you finish checking for each kind of error, place a check (✔) next to it on the list.

When you finish editing your own essay, exchange papers with a classmate and edit each other's work.

_____ 1. Basic sentence components

        Missing or repeated subject

        Missing verb

        Missing or repeated object /complement

_____ 2. Verbs

        Wrong verb tense

        Wrong verb form

_____ 3. Agreement

        No subject-verb agreement

        No agreement between a noun and its antecedent

_____ 4. Sentence boundaries

        Fragments

        Run-ons and comma splices

_____ 5. Spelling (*Hint*: To check spelling, read each line of words from right to left. This will help you see each word individually.)

Teacher's comments: _____

_____

_____

_____

_____

When you finish editing, attach this sheet to your draft.

WRITING SKILLS: PATTERNS OF ESSAY ORGANIZATION

English has two main patterns for organizing a comparative essay. To help you identify these patterns, here are two student drafts. As you read each one, think about how the writer organized the ideas. Both students wrote in response to Topic One of this project.

[1]When I came to United States, I had a lot of preconceived ideas. I thought I was stepping into paradise. I thought I was going to see a perfect country with happy people. I believed everyone had a comfortable life here. Unfortunately I observed different things that contradicted my ideas.

[2]Before I arrived I thought America is a neat and clean country. I saw many movies about America in my country and they always showed clean streets and clean houses and stores. I never saw dirt or garbage. But on the day of my arrival, I saw the opposite of that. I found this city especially is very dirty. There is garbage everywhere, not only in the street but also in the public places. When I go into the subway, I cannot stay there more than a few minutes because of the bad smells, piles of trash, and overflowing garbage cans. In fast food restaurants, I cannot find a clean area to sit and enjoy my food and they don't have clean restrooms.

[3]Second, I had the expectation that everyone here wore fashionable and glamorous clothes. The actresses in the American movies and the people in the American magazine pictures that I saw in my country always wore fancy dresses and suits that showed they had a lot of money and a comfortable life. But now I see that is not true. Most people, in fact, don't follow the latest fashion. They just wear any clothes they like. For example, some women wear jump suits or even clothes that look like pyjamas for shopping or going out. In my country, Iran, people always wore clothes that allowed you to know what their job was or where they were going. But most people here don't care about their clothes and they wear the same kind of clothes everywhere.

[4]Now I have learned America is very different from the picture in my mind. In truth, I didn't step into paradise.

To get a better picture of how this student organized the ideas, read the essay again and make an outline of the essay by filling in the chart that follows.

Paragraph 1: Introduction

Paragraph 2: Point 1 _____

    Side A (before): _____

Side B (after): _____

Paragraph 3: Point 2 _____

Side A (before): _____

Side B (after): _____

Paragraph 4: Conclusion

Here is a second student's draft written in response to Topic One. Remember as you read it to think about how the writer organized the ideas.

[1]America is really not same as I thought before I came here. My ideas about America had a big change after I came to live in this country.

[2]Before I came to the United States, I got much information about America from TV, movies, and newspapers. These formed a picture in my mind. I thought everyone was very friendly in America. They always smiled. They seldom argued with others and they always said good words to others. Also I thought everyone was very rich. There were many cars and high buildings. Everyone wore nice clothes and every home had electricity. Living in America was very easy, I thought, because the people who came back to China from the United States always said they lived very well in America. When they came home, they all brought many high cost goods that showed they earned money very easily. But in my mind, America was also a very dangerous place. There were a lot of murderers and bank robbers and other problems such as drugs and AIDS in America. I thought the crime rate was so high that people could be killed at any time.

[3]However, after I lived in America for two years, my opinions about America changed a lot. I realized that not everyone is friendly in America. Many Americans don't like foreign people. Although they are polite to foreigners, they don't really care about them in their heart. Also not everyone is very rich. There are many beggars on the street, and behind the beautiful high buildings there are many poor houses. In addition, living in America is not easy. I am unaccustomed to the food, the clothing, and the thinking, talking and actions of Americans, and there are few work chances for foreigners, so it is not easy to earn money here. But America is not as dangerous as I thought it. If people are careful and protect themselves, I think living in America is as safe as living in other countries in the world.

[4]Between my preconceptions and the reality of America, I found many differences. Now I would like to learn more about this country.

To get a better picture of the pattern of organization, look at the essay again and fill in the following chart.

Paragraph 1: Introduction

Paragraph 2: Side A (before): _____

Points 1. _____

        2. _____

        3. _____

        4. _____

Paragraph 3: Side B (after): _____

Points 1. _____

        2. _____

        3. _____

        4. _____

Paragraph 4: Conclusion

Did you notice the difference in organization in these two essays? The first student divided the information by using one paragraph to discuss each point or topic she wanted to discuss. For each point she presented both sides of the comparison, that is, her thoughts about the United States before she came and after she came. This method of organizing information is called a *point-by-point comparison*.

The second student, in contrast, divided the information into two blocks (in this case, two paragraphs) representing the two sides of the comparison, and then for each block or side he presented his points. First he discussed all the ideas he held about the United States before he came here, and then he discussed what he thought after his arrival. This method of organizing information is called a *block comparison* or a *side-by-side comparison*.

Point-by-point and side-by-side are two different methods of organizing a comparison-contrast essay. Both are equally valid ways of organizing your ideas; which method you choose will depend on the subject of your essay, how much you know about the subject, the length of your essay, and what you want your readers to remember. For some assignments, one method of organizing your ideas will work better. For other assignments, either method will be appropriate.

WRITING SKILLS: WRITING THE INTRODUCTION

To learn what a good introduction is, let's look at some introductory paragraphs. The three introductions that follow were written by three different students. They were all writing about the same topic: "What makes writing difficult?" Read each introduction and think about what it tells you.

1.   I agree with this statement for several reasons.

What do you think the rest of this essay will be about? _____

_____

_____

2.   Everybody learns to speak their native language well, but many people are not good writers. We learn to speak when we are very young. Our parents teach us. But we don't learn to write until we go to school.

What do you think the rest of this essay will be about? _____

_____

_____

3.   In today's modern world, writing and speaking are important skills in everybody's life. Both are necessary for social and economic success. But while most people can speak well enough to meet all their needs, many find it hard to write. They say they can write letters to their friends without problems, but when they must write for academic or work purposes, they cannot do it well. Why is this so?

What do you think the rest of this essay will be about? _____

_____

_____

Comparing these three paragraphs, which do you think a native speaker would consider a better introduction to the essay? _____

Why? _____

_____

_____

   Look at two more introductions. The two paragraphs were written in response to the same topic: "My Feelings When I First Arrived." Again, read each introduction and think about what it tells you.

1.   When I first came to America, I was very upset about the new language and different customs. Also I got homesick for my family and friends.

What do you think the rest of this essay will be about? _____

_____

_____

2. If anyone asks me what loneliness, nervousness, and homesickness mean, I can tell them. When I came to the United States, I experienced all these feelings. They are feelings I will never forget.

What do you think the rest of this essay will be about? _____

_____

_____

Comparing these two paragraphs, which would a native English speaker consider a better introduction to this essay? _____

Why? _____

_____

_____

Think about the better paragraph from each set of introductions. Why are they better? What do you think are the characteristics of a good introduction?

_____

_____

_____

_____

_____

_____

What Makes a Good Introduction?

A good introduction generally does three things:

> It informs
>
> It focuses
>
> It generates interest

1.   *It informs.* The introduction lets the reader know generally what the topic of the essay will be. Is the writer going to discuss writing, the death penalty, or television? Readers want to know so they can begin to think about this topic in relation to their own knowledge and experience.

2.   *It focuses.* The introduction tells the reader specifically what the main idea of the essay is. It focuses the reader's attention on the single most important idea that the writer will discuss in the rest of the essay.

　　In academic writing, readers expect to find the main idea clearly stated in the introduction. They feel confused if the introduction does not meet their expectation. In more literary writing, however, the main idea might not come until the end of the essay or it might not be directly stated at all.

3.   *It generates interest.* The introduction tries to catch the reader's attention and get the reader interested in what follows. If the introduction has interesting ideas or is written in an interesting style, the reader will be encouraged to go on and read the essay. If, however, the introduction is dull, the reader will probably lose interest or think the rest of the essay will be dull, too, and will look for excuses to avoid reading it.

Developing and Organizing the Introduction

You have probably been wondering how to improve the introductions to your essays. Here are some commonly asked questions and some answers and suggestions to help you.

1.   *How do I let my readers know what my topic is and at the same time write an interesting introduction?*

There are many ways to inform your readers and catch their attention.

- You can provide some interesting and appropriate facts about the topic.
- You can describe a general situation that your readers can relate to.
- You can describe a personal experience related to the topic.
- You can use a quotation from someone famous or expert in the subject.
- You can ask a thought-provoking question about the topic.
- You can make an unusual or surprising statement.

　　For example, look back at Laura Waterbury's essay on pages 38–39. She states her topic and main idea directly in two sentences in her first paragraph. Though this can be a boring way to begin, her statement is so personal and unusual that it gets the readers interested. Next, look at Amy Tan's essay on pages 54–55. She, too, uses personal information to get her readers interested, but she discusses her topic—language—more extensively; she also uses an unusual statement—that she grew up with and uses "all [her] Englishes." Lastly, look at Amparo Ojeda's essay that begins this project. To introduce her topic and involve her readers, she writes a detailed account of an experience she had as a child.

2.   *Is the main idea always stated in one sentence in the introduction?*

No. The main idea is often stated in a single sentence, especially in academic writing. But it can also be spread over several sentences or even an entire paragraph. And sometimes there is no main idea statement in the introduction at all.

3.   *Where do I put the main idea statement in the introduction? Does it go at the beginning, the middle, or the end?*

Again, there is no rule. However, many writers choose not to state the main idea in the first sentence of the introduction. Instead, they prefer to place it at or toward the end of the introduction because in that position it leads more directly into the body of the essay where the main idea is discussed. But remember: there is no single formula for good writing.

4.   *In addition to stating my main idea, should I also tell the reader what supporting points I will discuss?*

It depends on what you are writing and for whom. Academic writers commonly do this in formal essays and research papers written for their colleagues. Students often do it in exams when they have little time to be creative. However, writers of more literary or personal essays usually do not mention their supporting ideas until the body.

5.   *How long should the introduction be?*

Most writers try to balance the introduction and the rest of the essay. An essay that has a long introduction and a short body will seem top-heavy, and an essay that has a short introduction and a long body may seem out of balance as well.

However, it is possible to write an interesting introduction that is very short (as Laura Waterbury did); it is also possible to write a good introduction that is long. The best rule is: the introduction must be long enough to be effective. More practice in reading and writing introductions will help you judge.

Judging Introductions

Now that you have a better idea of what an introduction should do, look at the paragraphs that follow. The topic is the same as it was earlier: "What Makes Writing Difficult?" Read each paragraph and decide how successful you think the writer has been in reaching the goals of a good introduction.

1.   Writing has always been a difficult skill for me. I have never liked to write although I have been writing since I started school. Now I can tell how necessary it is to a person's life.

2. Writing is very important for our life, so we learn how to write in school. But writing is very difficult. We have to spend a lot of time on it, and speaking is easier than writing.

3. When I lived in Iran, I took a writing class in the ninth grade. The teacher never really taught us how to write. She never explained to us why it is important to our life to write. Instead, every time that she came to class, she told some students to read their compositions out loud. At the beginning I was not a good writer so I felt very nervous whenever she asked me. But she made writing seem an important subject, so I worked hard at it. I learned to like to write, and I also learned to write better. But I still think writing is very difficult.

4. Most students say that writing is more difficult than other language skills. They can speak, read, and understand what they hear without problem, but they have difficulty writing essays and research papers. I agree. I think academic writing is difficult because it is hard to find appropriate ideas to write about; it is difficult to express those ideas clearly and sufficiently; and it is hard to organize them in a way that makes sense to readers.

Which introductions do you think a native speaker would say are the most successful? _____

Why? _____

_____

_____

_____

_____

_____

_____

Improving the Introduction in Your Writing

Look back at the essays you have written so far. Choose one whose introduction you are not satisfied with and rewrite the introductory paragraph. Write as many drafts as necessary to get an introduction that informs, focusses, and generates interest. When you have finished, clip all the drafts of your new introduction to the original essay and hand them in.

WRITING SKILLS: ACHIEVING COHERENCE

In Project 1 we discussed how an English essay (and paragraph) limits itself to one controlling idea. You will recall that we called this feature *unity*, and we stressed how important it is to good writing. Then in Project 2 we looked at how English writers *develop* their ideas and we stressed the importance of developing ideas sufficiently. But unity and development are not the only characteristics of good writing. In this section we will examine another aspect of good writing.

In the two paragraphs that follow, the writer explains why he sometimes prefers to write letters to his friends rather than to call them on the telephone. At first glance the two paragraphs may seem identical, but if you read carefully and compare them, you will find some differences. Underline all the differences.

Paragraph A	Paragraph B
Sometimes I write letters to my friends in my country. It's more convenient for me to make phone calls. Sometimes I have words and feelings that can't be expressed well enough on the phone. I write.	Sometimes I write letters to my friends in my country. Although it's more convenient for me to make phone calls, sometimes I have words and feelings that can't be expressed well enough on the phone. So I write.

Which paragraph would a native speaker consider better writing? _____

Why? _____

_____

_____

In this next pair of paragraphs the writer describes one of the ways she has changed since she came to the United States. Again read both passages carefully and compare them. Underline all the differences you find.

Paragraph A	Paragraph B
1 Before I came here, I, like other 2 people in Taiwan, seldom gave my 3 two children praise since they did 4 a good job. However, I would try to 5 find some fault with them. I did 6 this because I thought if I gave 7 them too much praise they would 8 become proud and stop improving.	Before I came here, I, like other people in Taiwan, seldom gave my two children praise even though they did a good job. Instead, I would try to find some fault with them. I did this because I thought if I gave them too much praise they would become proud and stop

9 Next, after I came to the United
10 States, I always heard parents
11 telling their children, "I'm proud of
12 you." "You did a good job." I
13 wondered what the difference was
14 between the two and I started
15 praising my children instead of
16 criticizing. I felt very unsure of
17 myself after I was making this
18 change. Therefore, after I
19 compared the results of the two
20 approaches, I decided praising is a
21 better way to encourage a child
22 than criticizing.

improving. But after I came to the
United States, I always heard
parents telling their children, "I'm
proud of you." "You did a good job."
I wondered what the difference was
between the two so I started
praising my children instead of
criticizing. I felt very unsure of
myself while I was making this
change. However, after I compared
the results of the two approaches,
I decided praising is a better way
to encourage a child than
criticizing.

Again, which paragraph do you think a native speaker would consider better

writing? _____

Why? _____

_____

_____

You are probably beginning to recognize better writing, but can you describe what made these passages better? In the language of writing, we say that these passages have *coherence*. Coherence is another important characteristic of good writing. In a coherent passage, all the ideas follow one another logically and smoothly. The ideas develop in a way that allows the reader to easily follow the writer's thoughts through the paragraph and the essay. A coherent text makes sense to the reader.

If the writing lacks coherence—if the sentences do not fit together in the way the reader expects and the ideas are not logically and clearly connected— English readers cannot easily understand the writer's message and they feel frustrated.

Using Logical Connectors

One way that all good writers make their writing more coherent is by using *logical connectors*. These are words or phrases that show the relationship between ideas. Logical connectors are like road signs for the reader. They tell the reader how the information in one sentence or clause is linked to the information in another part of the same sentence, in another different sentence, or in another paragraph.

Logical connectors show four basic relationships between ideas. The table that follows illustrates these relationships.

RELATIONSHIP	EXPLANATION	EXAMPLES
1. Addition	Addition connectors add an idea, emphasize an idea, show that one idea is like another, or show an example.	*also* *in fact* *similarly* *for example*
2. Difference	Difference connectors show that two ideas are different or contradictory or that one idea replaces another idea.	*although* *in contrast*
3. Sequence	Sequence connectors show the order of ideas.	*first* *next*
4. Cause/ Effect (Reason/ Result)	Cause/effect connectors show that one idea is the reason, purpose, or condition for another idea, or that one idea is the result or effect of another idea.	*because* *so that* *if* *therefore* *so*

To show how logical connectors link ideas, here is an essay about the problems many foreign students face on American campuses. The essay includes a number of common logical connectors; they are shown in italics.

1   American colleges and universities recruit foreign students *because* they
2   help to increase enrollment, especially of students who pay tuition. For-
3   eigners *also* bring an international viewpoint and a sense of prestige to the
4   campus, *and* most of them are highly motivated and do well in their
5   courses. *Hence*, both the number of institutions enrolling foreign students
6   and the number of students studying here has increased dramatically in
7   the last five years. *However*, this development is not without problems.
8   Many foreign students complain the schools don't help them adjust to
9   life in America. They say they get no aid in dealing with the new customs,
10 they aren't prepared for the hostility they sometimes face on campus, *and*
11 they get no help adjusting to the new atmosphere in the classroom. *Indeed*,
12 some students say that even the orientation sessions and campus tours
13 offered to foreign students are confusing, especially for students who have
14 just stepped off an airplane after an 18-hour trip. *As a result*, they must rely
15 on each other for advice about everything from academic schedules to
16 American culture. They say that they experience culture shock and a sense
17 of alienation in classrooms and dormitories *and* that these problems last
18 through all their years at school.
19   Campus officials say they recognize the need to help foreign students
20 feel comfortable on campus, *and* they defend their efforts to help them ad-

21   just. They point to programs that they have developed to help the students
22   register for classes, improve their English and become familiar with Ameri-
23   can customs. *But* administrators say foreign students do not always take
24   advantage of the resources. *Instead of* mixing with Americans *so that* they
25   can practice the language and learn more about the culture, they tend to
26   stick together.
27   *Nonetheless*, some administrators agree that institutions have not done
28   enough to make foreign students feel welcome, *and* increasingly they are
29   looking for new and better ways to help students adjust. *In addition*, at
30   many campuses foreign students themselves are beginning to establish
31   programs to help new arrivals feel more at home.

Decide how each logical connector in the essay joins the ideas. What kind of relationship does it show? List the connectors in the appropriate column in the following table.

ADDITION	DIFFERENCE	SEQUENCE	CAUSE/EFFECT

Look back at other readings that you have done for this course and find the logical connectors. What kinds of relationships do they show? Add them to the table. Can you think of any more logical connectors you could add to the column in the table?

Importance of Logical Connectors

To see how logical connectors can make a passage easier for readers to follow, look back at the sample paragraphs on page 117. In the first set, in paragraph

A, no connectors are used and the reader is left to guess about the relationships between ideas. In paragraph B, in contrast, the writer uses connectors to make the logical relationships between the ideas clearer.

Now look at the second pair of paragraphs on pages 117–118. Both include logical connectors, but in paragraph A the connectors are misleading. They signal the reader to expect a certain logical relation between the ideas, but the relation that actually exists is different. They are false road signs that send the reader off in the wrong direction and cause confusion. In paragraph B, in contrast, the connectors are appropriate. The relationships they signal actually exist in the ideas. As a result, the ideas fit together in a way that makes sense to the reader, and the reader can more easily understand the passage.

Practice Using Difference Connectors

EXERCISE 1

The passages below need connectors to show the difference between the ideas. Add the connector shown in parentheses and change or add any punctuation necessary.

1. I have tried salad many times. I still don't like it. (but)

2. I keep trying to improve my English pronunciation. Many people still cannot understand me. (however)

3. I have been in this country only a few months. I already feel at home here. (yet)

4. I have visited this country several times before. This is the first time I am actually living here. (although)

5. In Japan, I always took off my shoes when I entered someone's home. Here I never take off my shoes when I go inside. (while)

EXERCISE 2

Complete each sentence with a differing or contrasting idea.

1. Life here is very exciting. *However,* _____

   _____

2. *Although* I have been studying here for two years, _____

   _____

3. I have tried to make American friends, *but* _____

   _____

4. *While* I agree that this country offers many opportunities for my education and career, _____

   _____

5. In my country only a very small number of students can go to university. *In contrast,* _____

_____

Notice that connectors showing the same logical relationship can follow different grammar rules. Connectors can be adverbs; they can be coordinating conjunctions (joining independent clauses); they can be subordinating conjunctions (beginning dependent clauses); and they can even be prepositions.

EXERCISE 3

The following is an essay that a student wrote about becoming Americanized. The flow of ideas could be improved by adding connectors to show difference. Read it and add appropriate connectors to make the meaning clearer.

1   Many young people who come to live in this country quickly become
2   Americanized. They start to act and think like Americans and they give up all
3   their own customs and traditions. I don't think I have become Americanized. I,
4   too, have changed in some ways and adopted some American customs.

5   The biggest change is my clothes. In my country, Afghanistan, except for the
6   time I was in school, I always wore my national dress. When I came home from
7   school in the afternoon, I put it on, and on weekends and holidays when I didn't
8   go to school, I wore it all day. Here I wear American style clothes most of the
9   time. I put on jeans or pants and a shirt every day, even when I am not going to
10 school. I wear my national dress only on Afghan holidays and when I go to the
11 mosque.

12 Also I am not as sensitive as I was in my country. In Afghanistan I always
13 tried to be helpful to people who had problems. I used to help poor people or give
14 money to beggars. In this country I realize that somebody needs help. I don't
15 care about him or help him. Here I have never helped or given money to
16 homeless people.

17 Another difference is my social life. In my country boys and girls go to
18 separate schools and teenagers do not go out on dates. Before I came here, I
19 never talked to girls alone and I never went out with a girl alone. Here I go to
20 school with girls. I see them and talk to them every day and I even went out
21 with a girl a while ago.

22   In general, I don't think I have really changed. I think inside I am still

23   Afghani. In fact, I am sure I will never completely adopt American ways of

24   thinking and behaving because I always want to be a real Afghani. I love my

25   country, my people, my traditions, and my religion.

Abdul Waheed Ayazi

Learning More about Logical Connectors

You can expand your repertoire of logical connectors by looking for them in your reading and by trying to use them in your writing. Whenever you see one in a passage, note how it is used. Look closely at the context. Even though many connecting words or phrases signal the same relationship, they may not be interchangeable. They may have slightly different meanings or they may fit only certain situations. Some connectors are more likely to be used in formal contexts, and others in informal contexts.

In your own writing, if you are not sure that a particular connector is appropriate, ask your teacher. With practice, you will learn what fits and what does not.

How Often Should Logical Connectors Be Used?

Although connecting words and phrases help the reader to follow your ideas, it is not good to use them in every sentence. Using too many connectors pulls the reader's attention away from your real ideas and breaks up the flow of your sentences.

Overusing connectors can also produce "stringy" sentences—sentences that are like strings of beads, with too many independent clauses held together with connectors. In the following paragraph, all the connectors are underlined. Note how "stringy" the last two sentences are.

In the Soviet Union I had studied German, <u>so</u> when I came here I didn't know any English. The first time I went to the supermarket somebody came up to me <u>and</u> asked the price of something, <u>but</u> I didn't understand what she was talking about, <u>so</u> I didn't answer her <u>and</u> I am sure she thought that I was really stupid <u>because</u> my face looked totally blank. Often during my first year here people talked to me <u>and</u> I couldn't understand them, <u>so</u> I didn't answer <u>and</u> I felt very embarrassed <u>and</u> I hated my life here.

There is no rule about the right number of connectors. Again, look at what experienced writers do and try to include at least some connectors in your own writing. With practice, you will begin to see where they help the reader to follow your ideas and where they are unnecessary or distracting.

Improving the Use of Difference Connectors in Your Writing

Look through the writing you have done up to now. Look for any paragraphs in which you expressed a contrast or difference between ideas but did not include any connectors (leaving the reader to guess the relationship) or you used a connector that sent the wrong signal; or you chose the same connector over and over (dull!). Using a different color pen or pencil, add difference connectors where necessary to make the ideas flow more clearly, or change any connectors that you have misused or used repetitively.

Ordering Ideas

Another important feature of coherent writing is the *order* in which the ideas are presented to the reader. The ideas must be sequenced in such a way that the reader can follow easily. For example, look at the two paragraphs that follow. Read them carefully and compare them.

Paragraph A

1 If you go to Kennedy
2 International Airport right now,
3 you will see lots of people still
4 immigrating to America. Perhaps
5 they have all different kinds of
6 dreams and plans about their
7 new homeland. I was one of them
8 about two years ago. However,
9 after living here awhile most
10 people realize that this is not the
11 same country that they have
12 dreamed about. I also had many
13 different thoughts about the
14 United States at that time. I
15 thought America was a peaceful
16 country, that educational
17 expenses were lower than in other
18 countries, and everyone had a fun
19 life. But I also had to change my
20 ideas after I came here.

Paragraph B

If you go to Kennedy International Airport right now, you will see lots of people still immigrating to America. Perhaps they have all different kinds of dreams and plans about their new homeland. After living here awhile, however, most immigrants realize that this is not the same country that they have dreamed about. I was one of those newcomers about two years ago. I also had many different thoughts about the United States at that time. I thought America was a peaceful country, that educational expenses were lower than in other countries, and everyone had a fun life. But I also had to change my ideas after I came here.

What differences did you find? _____

_____

Which paragraph would a native speaker consider better writing? _____

Why? _____

_____

_____

_____

Practice Improving the Order of Ideas

In the paragraph below, the writer discusses how her opinion of divorce has changed since she came to this country. However, the passage is organized in a way that is confusing to an English reader. Rearrange the sentences so the ideas are easier to follow. Rewrite the paragraph in the space provided.

[1]In Taiwan, I used to think that a married couple who didn't love each other any more had better not divorce if they had children. [2]Now I have changed and think divorce is acceptable if a couple doesn't love each other any more. [3]The couple doesn't have to maintain the marriage unwillingly because of their children. [4]They have a right to start a new life. [5]Before, in my mind, no matter how badly the couple got along, they had a responsibility to their children to stay together. [6]Even if they didn't love each other, they still had to give their children a home that included a father and mother.

_____

_____

_____

_____

_____

_____

_____

_____

_____

_____

_____

_____

_____

_____

Here is another paragraph with coherence problems. The writer describes his feelings about the climate, but he jumps back and forth between ideas. Re-arrange the sentences so the ideas are easier to follow. You may have to re-phrase some sentences to avoid repetition or add words or connectors to make the meaning clearer. Rewrite the paragraph in the space provided.

¹Another reason I hate living here is the climate. ²The weather is unpleasant most of the time because it is cold. ³Only four months of the year are warm. ⁴In my country it is very different. ⁵In the city where I lived, it is always warm and this country is always cold. ⁶Only in the summer is it warm, and also I don't like to wear a jacket, so I am unhappy most of the time.

_____

_____

_____

_____

_____

_____

_____

_____

SUGGESTED JOURNAL TOPICS

1.   Maria Gillan came to the United States from Italy as a child. The following poem, "Public School No. 18: Paterson, New Jersey," is about her experience in elementary school.

° **opaque:** not allowing light to pass through

Miss Wilson's eyes, opaque°
as blue glass, fix on me:
"We must speak English.
We're in America now."
I want to say, "I am American,"

° **stacked:** piled up

but the evidence is stacked° against me.

° **scalp:** skin on top of the head

My mother scrubs my scalp° raw, wraps
my shining hair in white rags
to make it curl, Miss Wilson
drags me to the window, checks my hair

° **lice:** small insects that live on warm-blooded animals, sometimes on humans

for lice.° My face wants to hide.

° **chatter:** talk a lot and quickly

At home, my words smooth in my mouth,
I chatter° and am proud. In school,
I am silent, grope for the right English
words, fear the Italian word

° **sprout:** grow

will sprout° from my mouth like a rose,

° **sprigged:** flowered

fear the progression of teachers
in their sprigged° dresses,
their Anglo-Saxon faces.

Without words, they tell me
to be ashamed.
I am.

° **booted:** shaped like a boot

I deny that booted° country
even from myself,
want to be still
and untouchable
as these women
who teach me to hate myself.

Choose a phrase or sentence from the poem that expresses your own feelings or thoughts. Write about it.

2. Saying Goodbye Is Really Hard

3. Unfriendly Americans

4. Reread the essay on pages 119–120 about the problems of foreign students. Do you think your school is doing enough to help you adjust to your new life here? What suggestions do you have?

5.

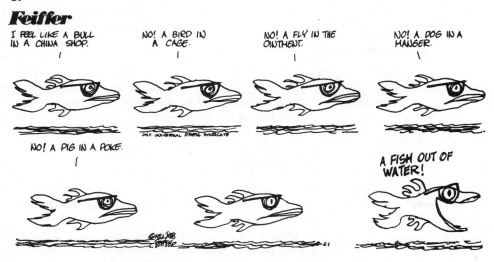

Feiffer copyright Jules Feiffer. Reprinted with permission of Universal Press Syndicate. All rights reserved.

Do you, too, feel like "a fish out of water"?

6. There is a proverb that says, "In seeking great happiness, small pleasures may be lost." How does this apply to your experience in coming to this country?

7. Judith Ortiz Cofer remembers her first years in the United States.

° **slate:** gray (like the rock called slate)
° **hues:** colors

My memories of life in Paterson [New Jersey] during those first few years are all in shades of gray. Maybe I was too young to absorb vivid colors and details, or to discriminate between the slate° blue of the winter sky and the darker hues° of the snow-bearing clouds, but that single color washes

° **slush:** partly melted snow

over the whole period. The building we lived in was gray, as were the streets, filled with slush° the first few months of my life there. The coat my father had bought for me was similar in color. . . .

What color do you remember most from your first days here?

8. Write a letter to a friend in your native country and tell him or her what life is like in this country and whether or not you recommend that he or she come to live here.

9. "As the traveler who has once been from home is wiser than he who has never left his own doorstep, so a knowledge of another culture should sharpen our ability to scrutinize more steadily, to appreciate more lovingly, our own" (Margaret Mead, American anthropologist, 1901-1978). What do you "appreciate more lovingly" about your own culture now that you live in another culture?

10. The American poet Robert Frost defined *home* as " . . . the place where, when you have to go there, they have to take you in." What is your definition of home?

11. How does it feel
To be on your own
With no direction home
Like a complete unknown
Like a rolling stone?

This verse is from "Like a Rolling Stone," a song by Bob Dylan (1941–   ), an American songwriter and performer. Write an answer in song or poetry form.

12. Voltaire, a French philosopher (1694–1778), said, "Paradise is where I am." Where is your paradise?

13. Amy Tan grew up in a Chinese family in California. Her first novel, *The Joy Luck Club*, was very popular and was made into a movie. In this excerpt from the book, one of the characters describes her experience of inviting her American boyfriend, Rich (short for Richard), to her parents' home for dinner.

° **frosted glasses:** glasses with a rough surface so you can't see through the glass
° **splayed:** spread out
° **knock-kneed:** having knees that turn inward and touch
° **Shoshona:** the narrator's young daughter

° **morsel:** very small piece
° **tender:** soft, easy to bite through
° **plucked:** picked or pulled sharply
° **sprouts:** very young plants

He had brought a bottle of French wine, something he did not know my parents could not appreciate. My parents did not even own wineglasses. And then he also made the mistake of drinking not one but two frosted glasses° full, while everybody else had a half-inch "just for taste."

When I offered Rich a fork, he insisted on using the slippery ivory chopsticks. He held them splayed° like the knock-kneed° legs of an ostrich while picking up a large chunk of sauce-coated eggplant. Halfway between his plate and his open mouth, the chunk fell on his crisp white shirt and then slid into his crotch. It took several minutes to get Shoshona° to stop shrieking with laughter.

And then he had helped himself to big portions of the shrimp and snow peas, not realizing he should have taken only a polite spoonful, until everybody had had a morsel.°

He had declined the sautéed new greens, the tender° and expensive leaves of bean plants plucked° before the sprouts° turn into beans. And Shoshona refused to eat them also, pointing to Rich: "He didn't eat them! He didn't eat them!"

He thought he was being polite by refusing seconds, when he should have followed my father's example, who made a big show of taking small portions of seconds, thirds, and even fourths, always saying he could not

° **groaning:** making a loud sound of suffering

° **disparaging:** making someone or something sound of little value or importance

° **cue:** signal (to speak or act)
° **proclaim:** declare, say boldly
° **platter:** large, flat dish for serving food

resist another bite of something or other, and then groaning° that he was so full he thought he would burst.

But the worst was when Rich criticized my mother's cooking, and he didn't even know what he had done. As is the Chinese cook's custom, my mother always made disparaging° remarks about her own cooking. That night she chose to direct it toward her famous steamed pork and preserved vegetable dish, which she always served with special pride.

"Ai! This dish not salty enough, no flavor," she complained, after tasting a small bite. "It is too bad to eat."

This was our family's cue° to eat some and proclaim° it the best she had ever made. But before we could do so, Rich said, "You know, all it needs is a little soy sauce." And he proceeded to pour a riverful of the salty black stuff on the platter,° right before my mother's horrified eyes. . . .

Think about your own culture, and what a foreigner should know about your eating customs to avoid embarassment. (Think carefully because you probably are so used to your own customs that they seem natural to you.) Pretend that you have invited an American friend to your parents' home for dinner. Write a letter to your friend describing your culture's eating customs and tell your friend what he or she should and should not do.

14. Things Americans Do That Really Bother Me

15. Theodore Roosevelt, president of the United States from 1901–1909, said, "Every immigrant who comes here should be required within five years to learn English or leave the country." Do you agree?

16. Imagine that you are moving to a new country and will never return home. You can take with you only one medium-size suitcase. What will you put in it?

ADDITIONAL WRITING TOPICS

1. Many people experience culture shock when they move to another country. At first they find it difficult to become accustomed to the different way of life in the new country. How did you feel when you first came here and what caused these feelings? Do you still feel this way now?

2. Every ethnic group has its own customs, its own rules of behavior. Reread the essay by Amparo Ojeda on pages 92–94. What differences does she find between Filipinos and Americans in rules of behavior? What American customs have you found that are different from your own? How do you feel about these cultural differences?

3. In your native country, you probably had many friends; now that you have come to a new country, you have to build new friendships. Most newcomers hope to make at least some American friends, but often find that this is difficult to do. Write an essay about the importance and difficulty of making friends with English speakers. If possible, use your own experience to illustrate your essay.

ADDITIONAL READINGS

Maxine Hong Kingston. "The Misery of Silence." *The Woman Warrior: Memoirs of a Girlhood among Ghosts*. New York: Alfred A. Knopf, Inc. 1976. Reprinted in *Life Studies: A Thematic Reader,* 3rd ed. Edited by David Cavitch. New York: St. Martin's Press 1989.

Milos Vamos. "How I'll Become an American." *The New York Times*. April 17, 1989. Reprinted in *Patterns for College Writing*, 5th ed. Edited by Laurie G. Kirszner and Stephen R. Mandell. New York: St. Martin's Press 1992.

Alan Wolfe. "The Return of the Melting Pot." *The New Republic*. Dec. 31, 1990. Reprinted in *Side by Side: A Multicultural Reader*, pp. 450–451. Edited by Harvey S. Wiener and Charles Bazerman. Boston: Houghton Mifflin 1993.

Elizabeth Wong. "The Struggle to Be an All-American Girl." *The Los Angeles Times*, 1980. Reprinted in *The Short Prose Reader,* 5th ed., pp. 129–131. Edited by Gilbert H. Muller and Harvey S. Wiener. New York: McGraw-Hill 1989.

P R O J E C T
4

TEACHERS AND
LEARNERS

In this project, you will

- try another brainstorming method: clustering.
- think about what to say in the conclusion of an essay.
- continue to work on improving the coherence of your writing.
- write several assignments about teachers and learners.
- continue to practice critical reading and revision.
- continue to practice editing your writing.
- continue writing in your journal.

GETTING IDEAS

You have now tried three techniques to get your ideas down on paper: listing, free-writing, and asking wh– questions. Another method that writers use is called *clustering*.

Brainstorming Method 4: Clustering

A cluster is a small, close group of similar things. There can be a cluster of people, a cluster of stars or, as the word is used here, a cluster of closely related ideas. To cluster your ideas, begin with a blank sheet of paper. In the middle of the page, write the main question or topic you want to explore and circle it. Next, brainstorm this question or topic and in the space around it, write any related or supporting ideas that occur to you. Circle these words too, and draw lines connecting them to your main topic and to each other according to any relationships that you see. Then brainstorm again and write your thoughts about each supporting idea in the space that surrounds it.

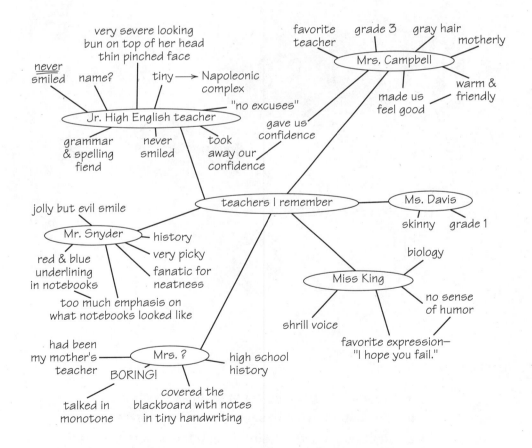

FIGURE 4–1. Example of clustering

As Figure 4–1 shows, clustering creates a series of wheels. There is one idea at the center or hub, and all the related ideas radiate out like the spokes of the wheel. Each sub-idea then becomes the hub of a new wheel.

In clustering, as in earlier brainstorming exercises, you write as fast as you can and write as many ideas as you can think of. There is no limit to the number of clusters (or wheels) you can create, and there is no right or wrong way to form the clusters. And again, you don't worry about spelling or grammar or try to make a sensible composition out of your clusters. Clustering is just a way to get ideas down on paper and begin thinking about your topic.

To begin this project, you are going to try clustering as a brainstorming technique.

Which Brainstorming Technique Is Best?

Is clustering better than the other brainstorming methods you have learned? No. It's just another possibility. Remember, there is no one correct way to get started. Each assignment is different. For some assignments, any of the brainstorming techniques may be suitable; for other assignments, one method may be more appropriate.

Also remember that each writer is different; each of you has your own way to write and you may find that one technique is more productive for you than another. The more you write, the more you will discover what works best for you.

But brainstorming in whatever way you choose is always a good way to get ideas about a topic before you start to write and to explore an idea further if you get stuck while you are writing.

STARTING TO THINK ABOUT THE TOPIC OF THIS PROJECT

Think about all the teachers you have had in your life—good ones, bad ones, mediocre ones. Which do you remember and what do you remember about them? Brainstorm for ten minutes. Write *teachers I remember* in the middle of this page and circle the phrase. Around your topic, write the names (or descriptions if you can't remember names) of the teachers you remember. Circle each name after you write it. Then, as ideas come to your mind about each teacher, write those ideas around the teacher's name.

Getting Ideas through Reading

1. When you were in high school, did you have any choice about the courses you could take?

2. Did you ever dislike a subject because you didn't like the teacher who taught it?

3. Did you ever have a teacher who got you interested in a subject that you thought you didn't like?

Tama Janowitz is a well-known American fiction writer. In this essay titled, "He Rocked, I Reeled," she writes about the teachers that she remembers and why she remembers them.

° **remedial:** a class to help students who are weak in a subject
° **juvenile delinquents:** young people who have broken the law

In high school, I took a remedial° English class—maybe it wasn't remedial, exactly, but without my knowing it, I had signed up for some kind of English class for juvenile delinquents.°

Well, it wasn't supposed to be a class for juvenile delinquents, but somehow everybody but me knew that was who it was for; maybe it was listed in the course catalog as being for those students in the commercial program, the general program, whatever it was called to distinguish it from the academic precollege preparation program.

° **surly:** bad-tempered and unfriendly
° **hair-dos:** hair styles

But anyway, on the first day I figured out who this course was directed at: The students were surly° and wore leather jackets, and the girls all had shag hair-dos° as opposed to straight and ironed, which was how the "nice" girls wore their hair.

Knowing me, I must have signed up for that class because it indicated that no work would be involved. And I was prepared for the worst, because somehow, having moved and switched schools so many times, I had been stuck in juvenile delinquent classes before.

° **contemptuous:** attitude of looking down on or disrespecting someone
° **sneering:** showing contempt by facial expression

The juvenile delinquent classes generally meant angry teachers and angry students who never read the books assigned and never spoke in class, which was no wonder because the teacher was generally contemptuous° and sneering.°

But this class ended up being different; the main thing was that the teacher, Mr. Paul Steele, didn't seem to know he was teaching students who weren't supposed to be able to learn. He assigned the books—by Sherwood Anderson, by Hemingway, by Melville—and somehow by the due date everyone had read them and was willing to talk about them.

° **distracted:** not paying close attention

Mr. Steele was a little distracted,° a little dreamy, and most excellent. It was one of the few times up until that age I had a teacher who spoke to me—and the rest of the class—with the honesty of one adult talking to others, without pretense or condescension;° there was no wrong or right, just discussion.

° **condescension:** feeling of superiority

In college, I had another great course—in geology, a subject for which I had no interest. Once again, I had signed up for something that looked easy, a "gut"° course to fulfill the science requirement.

° **gut:** slang for *easy*

But this guy—I believe his name was Professor Sand, an apt name for a geology teacher—was so excited and in love with rocks, with everything pertaining° to the formation of the earth, that to this day rocks and everything pertaining to the formation of the earth still get me excited.

° **pertaining:** related

Oolitic limestone, feldspar, gypsum, iron pyrite, Manhattan schist—the names were like descriptions of food, almost edible, and as around that time I was starting to become interested in writing, the enthusiasm that the teacher had for the subject was transferred to me into an enthusiasm for language.

And the names of the different periods—the Jurassic, the Pre-Cambrian—even though I can't remember much about them, the words still hold mystery and richness.

° **Catskills:** mountains in New York State

° **fossil:** hardened part or print of ancient animal or plant that is preserved in rock

° **millennia:** thousands of years

At the end of the semester, there was a field trip up to the Catskills,° to put into practice some of the techniques discussed in class. We were taken to a fossil° bed of trilobites where, due to the particular condition of the sedimentary bed, only the trilobite bodies had been preserved over the millennia.°

After a few minutes of listening to the professor's explanation, I bent over and picked up a piece of rock with a small lump sticking out of it and took it over to him.

To me, all I had found was a rock with a lump; but Professor Sand was totally amazed—I was the only one ever to find a fossilized trilobite complete with head.

° **bearing on:** relation to

Really, at that point there was little to stop me from becoming a geologist except for the fact that I knew I could never do anything involving numbers, weights, or measurements, which I suspected would at some point have some bearing on° the subject.

I remember another teacher, in graduate school, Francine du Plessix Gray, who taught a course called Religion and Literature—another subject in which I had no interest. But the way she spoke was so beautiful, in an accent slightly French-tinged. And because she was so interested in her topic, the students became interested, and her seminars were alive and full of argument.

Of course, I had many other fine teachers along the way, but the ones who stand out in my mind were those who were most enthusiastic about what they were teaching.

° **aloof:** apart; distant in feeling

° **pompous:** foolishly self-important

Many subjects in which I initially thought I was interested were totally destroyed for me by the teacher's dry, aloof,° pompous,° disengaged way of speaking.

But where the teacher was excited about the topic—as if he or she was still a little kid, rushing in from the yard to tell a story—that was when the subject became alive for me.

Getting More Ideas through Discussion

Now it is time to get more ideas by discussing the topic with your classmates. Discussing a subject with friends can be an excellent source of ideas, but remember that for discussion to be worthwhile you must really *listen* to each other and *question* each other.

Discuss each question as a group. Share all your thoughts, and write down all the ideas that are suggested. If you don't understand someone's idea, don't just assume it is your problem with English. Ask for clarification. Maybe the idea is not really clear to the person who offered it. Explore each other's thoughts; challenge each other's ideas.

Discussion Questions

1.   Have you ever tried to teach someone something? Describe the experience to your group (who, what, where, when). Were you successful? Why or why not?

NAME	EXPERIENCE (WHO/WHAT/WHERE/WHEN)	SUCCESS?

2.   What are the characteristics of a *good teacher*? Explain each quality as fully as you can.

QUALITY	EXPLANATION

QUALITY	EXPLANATION

3.   Think about the relationship between teaching and learning. Does teaching always produce learning? Does learning always require teaching? Or are they independent of each other? Free-write for ten minutes on this topic. When you finish, share your free-writing with your group.

_____

_____

_____

_____

_____

_____

_____

_____

_____

_____

_____

_____

_____

_____

_____

_____

_____

_____

_____

_____

ESSAY TOPICS FOR PROJECT 4

By now you should have many ideas on the subject of this project, so it is time to write. Choose one of the following topics about teachers.

1. Describe a teacher you had who made a significant impression on you—positive or negative. What did this person do that caused you to remember him or her for so many years? What did you learn from your experience in this teacher's class about the meaning of a *good teacher*?

2. What does the term *good teacher* mean? Describe the characteristics or qualities that define a good teacher. Then think about yourself. Do you think you could be a good teacher? Explain your answer.

PREWRITING

The first step is to get some ideas down on paper. Look back at the brainstorming, reading, and discussion earlier in the project for ideas you can use.

Brainstorming

Brainstorm for ten minutes on your chosen topic. Choose whichever technique you prefer: listing, free-writing, asking wh–questions, or clustering. Use a clean sheet of paper for your brainstorming. This is part of your project and you will hand it in later. Take this time to really explore your thoughts. As ideas come to you, include any facts, explanations or examples you could use to develop them.

Do you have any ideas for an introduction? If so, write the heading *Introduction* on a separate piece of paper and jot down your ideas. If not, don't worry and don't waste time staring into space. When you write your first draft, you can always start with the body of your essay and go back to the introduction later. Just because the introduction comes first in the essay doesn't mean you must actually write it first.

Do you have any ideas for a conclusion? If so, write *Conclusion* on a separate piece of paper and note down your ideas. If not, don't worry; something will probably come to you as you write your essay.

Outlining

If you feel it is useful to make an outline of your essay before you start writing, do so. Many writers find it helps them to focus their thoughts, plan their essay and organize their ideas. Remember, however, that writing is a process of discovering what you want to say. So if you make an outline beforehand, do not feel you must follow it absolutely. You can still change your mind as you write.

WRITING THE FIRST DRAFT

You are ready to write your first draft. If you have written an outline, use it as a guide. (An outline is only a skeleton of an essay; you must still develop the ideas into a full, coherent essay.) If you have only brainstormed, keep referring to your brainstorming notes as a source of ideas as you plan and write. If you run out of ideas at any point, brainstorm again on another piece of paper. Don't worry about minor grammatical errors, spelling, or how messy your paper looks (as long as it is readable). But do remember to double-space and write on one side of the page only.

When you have finished, read your essay from beginning to end. If you can find a place where you won't disturb anyone, read it aloud. Is there any part that doesn't sound right to you? Is there any part you would like to change? Did you suddenly think of more information you could add or a better way to explain an idea? Go ahead and make changes. Think of Draft One as a work in progress that is finished only when your time is up. Continue working until your instructor tells you to stop.

Clip together your draft and all your prewriting (your brainstorming and outlining, if you did any) and hand them in to your teacher.

BEFORE STARTING THE READER RESPONSE AND REVISION SECTIONS, TURN TO THE WRITING SKILLS SECTION BEGINNING ON PAGE 151.

READER RESPONSE

It is time to change hats and papers again and be a reader. Remember, your purpose is not to look for all the mistakes in your partner's writing but to give your views as a reader so your partner can improve his essay. Becoming a better reader of someone else's writing helps you learn to look at your own writing from a reader's viewpoint.

> In this project, you are going to look especially at the coherence of the writing and at the conclusion of the essay.

Reader Response Sheet 4

Draft written by _____

Draft read by _____

Read the entire essay. If you can't understand any part, underline it and put a question mark next to it.

Questions to Answer

1.   What do you think the writer's purpose is in this essay?_____

_____

2.   What is the writer's main idea? If it is directly stated, underline it and write it here.

If there is no statement of the main idea, tell the writer._____

_____

Is the main idea clearly stated? Do you fully understand it?_____

3.   Does the writer's purpose and main idea answer the assignment?

Yes _____   Partly _____   No_____   (If no, give the essay back to the writer.)

Organization and Development

On a clean sheet of paper, outline the essay. If the main idea of each paragraph is not clear or the paragraph needs more development, tell the writer.

Coherence

1.   Are there any places where the writer should add a connector or use a different connector to help you understand the relationship between ideas?

2.   Within each paragraph, do the ideas flow smoothly or are there big gaps between ideas?

3.   Does each paragraph connect smoothly to the one before?

Suggestions for improvement: _____

_____

_____

_____

_____

_____

Conclusion

Is there a conclusion?_____ If yes, is it successful?_____ (Does it give you the idea that the essay has ended? Does it take you back to the main idea of the essay? Is it as interesting as the rest of the essay?)

Suggestions for improvement:_____

_____

_____

_____

_____

When you finish, return this response sheet and the draft to the writer.

Example of a Student Essay

Here is the first draft of an essay that a student, Zhaoyan Lin, wrote in response to Topic Two. As you read it, think about how well the ideas interconnect with and follow each other and how successful the conclusion is. Then look at the Reader Response Sheet that follows the essay to see what one of Zhaoyan's classmates thought.

I like to teach others because it make me feel useful and knowledgeable. However, after some failed experience to teach, I don't think I could be a good teacher forever.

A good teacher must be patient. When student didn't understand and ask question, the teacher should be patient and happy to explain. A good teacher must consider and understand student's situation. When a student had some problems to learn, the teacher should care and help him/her to find what make it difficult.

But I could not become a good teacher. For example, I have been taught my sister to learn driving. I never thought she was afraid to drive. I pushed her to learn and wished her to be able to pass the driving test after one day's study. When she couldn't as good as I wish, I yelled to her. After a hour's study, she became very angry with me and swore that she would never learn driving from me. And I never tried to teach her driving again.

After several failed experience in teaching, now I find I am not able to become a good teacher. Who wish to learn things from a teacher like me!

Zhaoyan Lin

Example of a Reader Response

The following Reader Response Sheet shows how a classmate responded to Zhaoyan's essay.

Questions to Answer

1. What do you think the writer's purpose is in this essay?_____

To describe a good teacher and explain why the writer is not good teacher.

2. What is the writer's main idea? If it is directly stated, underline it and write it here. If there is no statement of the main idea, tell the writer. _____

I don't think I could be a good teacher forever

Is the main idea clearly stated? Do you fully understand it? __*yes*___

3. Does the writer's purpose and main idea answer the assignment?

Yes √____   Partly _____   No_____ (If no, give the essay back to the writer.)

Organization and Development

On a clean sheet of paper, outline the essay. If the main idea of each paragraph is not clear or the paragraph needs more development, tell the writer.

Coherence

1. Are there any places where the writer should add a connector or use a different connector to help you understand the relationship between ideas?

2. Within each paragraph, do the ideas flow smoothly or are there big gaps between ideas?

3. Does each paragraph connect smoothly to the one before?

Suggestions for improvement: *In paragraphs 1, 3, & 4, I follow easily your ideas from one sentence to next sentence. But paragraph 2 is not clear because you describe about more than one characteristic of good teacher in same paragraph. Maybe you need more general first sentence (better topic sentence?) and some connectors (e.g. first, second, also). Also you give good example in paragraph 3, but you need to show directly relation to paragraph 2. Reader shouldn't guess. In last paragraph, you write "several failed experiences," but in paragraph 3 you only say one.*

Conclusion

Is there a conclusion? _yes_ If yes, is it successful? _yes_ (Does it give you the idea that the essay has ended? Does it take you back to the main idea of the essay? Is it as interesting as the rest of the essay?)

Suggestions for improvement: _I like last sentence. I think its funny. But if you make description part of essay (longer body), maybe your conclusion will be too short. Do you still want to become a teacher? Maybe you can improve!_

REVISING YOUR DRAFT

The next step is to revise your draft. You will recall from Project One that revising does *not* mean just correcting your grammar and spelling. It does *not* mean just changing a word here and there. It does *not* mean just recopying Draft One more neatly. To revise means to think again about what you want to say and to rewrite parts or even all of your essay to make your ideas clearer and more convincing to your reader. Revising is a normal part of writing, not a punishment that teachers inflict on students who are bad writers. Successful writers will always tell you how much they rewrite.

> *My first draft usually has only a few elements worth keeping. I have to find out what those are and build from them and throw out what doesn't work.*
>
> SUSAN SONTAG

> *I do a lot of revising. Certain [parts] six or seven times. Occasionally you can hit it right the first time. More often you don't.*
>
> JOHN DOS PASSOS

Revision Questions

As you start Draft Two, think again about the goals you worked on in the previous projects. Ask yourself the following questions.

- What am I trying to do in this essay? What is my purpose? What main idea am I trying to communicate to my readers? Who are my readers? What do they need to know to understand?

- Do I have an introduction? Does it let my readers know what the essay will be about and get them interested?

- Is my essay unified? Is each paragraph unified? Have I included any information that moves too far away from my main idea or appears unrelated because I don't show how it is related?

- Have I developed my ideas sufficiently? Where do I need more or better information?

- Have I arranged the ideas in the best possible order?

In this fourth project you have two additional goals: to further improve the coherence of your writing and to improve the conclusion. Look at your reader's comments and ask yourself these questions.

1. *Does my conclusion let the reader know that the essay is ending? Does it take the reader back to the main idea? Is it interesting to read?*

To improve your conclusion, try rephrasing some of the sentences, adding more ideas, or rearranging the order of the ideas. Or if necessary, write a whole new paragraph.

2. *Is this piece of writing as coherent as I can make it?*

To improve the coherence of your essay, look very carefully at how you move from one sentence to the next. If there are logical gaps between the ideas, add phrases or clauses to bridge the gaps or rearrange the parts of the sentence to make the ideas flow more smoothly. Also check the connectors you use. Are they appropriate? Do you need to add some or eliminate some?

Remember, you can make changes directly on Draft One. It is not sacred. If you are writing by hand and have double-spaced, you can write in the blank lines or the margins. You can cross out words or sentences. You can cut the page up, reorder the parts you like, and staple or tape the pieces to another sheet of paper. You can add new ideas or new paragraphs by writing them on another sheet and using arrows or numbers to show where they should go. If you are writing on a word processor, work directly on the screen and print out a hard copy periodically. This method of revising helps you to see what you have changed and what you have kept. It also helps you to see if you are really revising or just making a few minor changes.

As you revise or after you have finished revising, make a list of all your revisions and attach it to your draft. Then reread what you have written. If possible, read your essay out loud. Listening to the sound of your writing can help you discover ideas that do not follow each other smoothly or words that repeat too often or are accidentally left out.

If there is any part of your essay that still doesn't sound right to you or satisfy you, revise some more. Continue working until you are satisfied or you run out of time.

Then check to see if your draft is legible. You are not finished with this project yet, so your draft does not have to be beautiful. But if large parts of your essay are no longer readable, you should write out a clean draft.

Example of a Student Revision

Reread the first draft of Zhaoyan's essay on page 143. Then read her second draft here. Notice how she uses some of her reader's suggestions and some of her own ideas in her revision.

[1]Everyone can teach others something. But to be a good teacher is very difficult. Not everyone can become a good teacher. It require special characteristics in a person. Unfortunately I don't have them.

[2]First a good teacher should be kind and considerate to students. She must consider students' own situation and care their feelings. When a student has the problems in learning, the teacher should talk with him/her and they work together to overcome the difficulties.

[3]Also a good teacher must be patient—as patient as a kindly father or mother to his/her children. When a student doesn't understand and asks some questions, the teacher should be happy to explain. She should never get angry if a student didn't learn quickly as she hoped.

[4]Many years ago I wished to become a teacher. I thought to successfully teach others would make me feel useful and knowledgeable. But after some failed experiences in teaching, I don't think I could be a good teacher now.

[5]One of my unpleasant teaching experiences happened last year. I tried to teach my sister driving a car. I never thought she was afraid to drive a car. So I pushed her to learn and asked her to be able to pass the driving test after one day's practice just as I did. When she couldn't do as good as I wished, I yelled to her. After one hour's study, she was nervous and became very angry with me. She said, "Why don't you think about the time you learned to drive? In the beginning, you couldn't do as perfect as you wish I do, too. I could never learn driving from you! You are too impatient and don't care me!" I was upset. I failed to be a good teacher because of impatient and careless.

[6]I had another failed experience in the past. When I was in high school, one day I tried to teach my classmate mathematics. I really had no idea why she didn't understand. After several times explain a question, I found she confused as the beginning. I lost my patience and did the whole homework for her.

[7]Now I know that being a good teacher is very difficult. I truly admire the people who are good teachers since I hardly can become one of them. Nevertheless maybe next time I would have another chance, I will try again. Maybe I can improve. Even I can't be a good teacher, I can be better than in the past.

Zhaoyan Lin

After Zhaoyan finished she made a list of her revisions.

1. I wrote a new introduction. It introduces whole essay and tells the main idea. I took the old introduction and I included it in new paragraph 4 which is like an introduction to second half of the essay, the part about my experience.

2. I divided paragraph 2 because I discussed two different points. Also I added more information to new paragraph 3.

3. In paragraph 5 (about teaching my sister driving), I added information about what she said. I tried to make the paragraph more interesting.

4. Paragraph 6 is a new paragraph about another failed experience. It is proving my point more that I am not a good teacher.

5. I wrote a new conclusion. I tried to relate to a more general idea and I tried to be not so negative.

BEFORE STARTING TO EDIT, TURN TO THE GRAMMAR SECTION ON PAGES 210–222.

EDITING

Until now, you have been concentrating on putting your ideas down on paper so they will be clear and convincing to your readers. You have been thinking about the whole piece of writing, its content and its organization. In the drafts you have written so far, you have been urged not to worry about grammar or spelling because you would have the opportunity to work on them later. Now it is time to edit your writing. Now you will look closely at grammar and spelling, and you will get help from your classmates and instructor just as you did when you revised your essay. Use the Editing Checklist on page 149 as a guide, and don't forget to edit in a different color pen or pencil.

Steps in Editing

1. Read your paper very carefully, checking for the errors listed on the Editing Checklist.

2. Exchange papers with a classmate, and read your partner's paper carefully looking for these same kinds of errors. By editing a classmate's paper, you not only help someone else but you also help train your own eye.

> You cannot correct every error you make, but if you learn to spot and correct at least the errors on your Editing Checklist, your readers will understand your ideas better and they will think more highly of your writing ability.

When you finish editing, clip together all parts of the project and give them to your teacher to check. When your essay is returned to you, remember to file it with the rest of your writing.

Editing Checklist 4

Draft checked by _____

     Read your own essay carefully several times, each time looking for and correcting one kind of error on the list below. As you finish checking for each type of error, place a check (✔) next to it on the list.

     When you finish editing your own essay, exchange papers with a classmate and edit each other's work.

_____ 1. Basic sentence components

       Missing or repeated subject

       Missing verb

       Missing or repeated object/complement

_____ 2. Verbs

       Wrong verb tense

       Wrong verb form

_____ 3. Agreement

       No subject-verb agreement

       No agreement between noun and its quantifier

_____ 4. Sentence boundaries

       Fragments

       Run-ons and comma splices

_____ 5. Pronouns

_____ 6. Punctuation

_____ 7. Spelling (*Hint:* To check spelling, read each line of words from right to left. This will help you see each word individually.)

Teacher's comments: _____

_____

_____

_____

_____

When you finish editing, attach this sheet to your draft.

WRITING SKILLS: WRITING THE CONCLUSION

The last part of an essay is the conclusion. Not every piece of writing has a separate concluding section, but most essays do, especially academic essays. The conclusion has two functions: to establish the idea that the essay has ended and to refocus the reader's attention on the main idea of the essay.

Importance of the Conclusion

By the time you have brainstormed and written your first draft, by the time you have struggled with your ideas and decided how best to say them, you are probably tired. It is difficult to maintain your enthusiasm for your topic in order to write a good ending. But the conclusion is one of the most important parts of the essay. Because it is the last thing the reader reads, it gives the reader a final impression of your essay.

What Makes a Good Conclusion?

Just as there are many ways to start an essay, there are many ways to end one. Here are some suggestions.

1.   Restate the major idea of the essay.

Either restate the main idea or summarize the main idea plus the supporting points. Amy Tan does this in her essay on pages 54–56. She begins by talking about how she uses many different kinds of English and how her mother's English came to influence her writing. She ends with the same idea. Donald Murray also uses this technique in his essay on pages 77–78. He begins by stating that professional writers view rewriting as essential to discovering what they really want to say and how best to say it, and he concludes by returning to this same point in his last paragraph.

Restating major ideas is the most traditional way to conclude, especially in an academic essay. But if it is not used imaginatively, it can be the most boring way to end, especially in a short essay where the main points stay fresh in the reader's mind. It can give the reader the impression that you have run out of ideas or are tired of the essay and are looking for the quickest way to finish. If you decide to conclude your essay by restating the major ideas, try to phrase your ideas in different words or use another technique in addition to restatement to add interest.

2.   Draw some implications from the ideas you have discussed.

Implications are conclusions or suggestions that you have not expressed directly in your essay but that develop logically from what you have said.

For example, look at Tama Janowitz's essay at the beginning of this chapter (pages 135–136). Most of her essay describes specific teachers she has had. But at the end, Janowitz draws out of these personal experiences some general thoughts about good teachers.

Laura Waterbury (pages 38–39) uses a similar technique. After she discusses specifically why and how she became an atheist, she ends by making more general statements about how atheism affects other areas of her life.

How could you use this approach? If you were writing about Topic One in this project you might conclude by inferring from your experience that there are many teachers who use some of the techniques you discuss, but few who use all of them. Or you might end with the inference that your struggle to explain *good* shows that the concept is difficult to define, but easier to recognize in practice. Or you could conclude by discussing that the fact you so clearly remember this teacher shows how influential a teacher can be.

If you were writing about Topic Two, you might conclude with the inference that even though you do not have the necessary characteristics to be a good teacher, you are good at other things; or that your lack of suitable qualities is not necessarily permanent and you could develop in the future; or that being good at some endeavor does not necessarily mean that you want to pursue it as a career.

3. Discuss your ideas in a larger context.

Context refers to the general conditions in which an event or action takes place. Thus, you can link your main idea to some future event or situation, or you can show how it is related to some broader issue.

For example, look at James Baker's essay classifying students (pages 159–60). He ends by discussing what he considers a real student (unlike the types he has described earlier), the kind of student he is always looking for, the student that reflects himself. In this way, he moves the essay from just a funny classification of students to a more serious commentary on students and learning.

In the conclusion to her essay (page 27), Azita Abishour, similarly moves from a discussion of her specific personality characteristics to the larger issue of changing herself.

How could you write this kind of conclusion? If you were writing about Topic One in this project, you could conclude by discussing the importance of teachers in general in society, and especially the importance of good teachers. Or you might end your essay by showing the relationship between your specific idea of a good teacher and more general ideas about excellence.

If you were writing about Topic Two, you might show the relation between yourself and the larger population—just as you would (or would not) make a good teacher, so would (or would not) most people you know. Or because society needs teachers, you might suggest in your conclusion that people who really like to teach should teach even though they will never be memorable teachers.

Some Concluding Thoughts about Conclusions

As you can see, there are numerous ways to conclude an essay. How you choose to end a particular piece of writing will depend on why you are writing it, whom you are writing for, how much time you have for writing, and your own experience and knowledge.

But don't be alarmed if by the time you get to the conclusion your brain feels like a sponge that has been wrung out and you can't think of an interesting way to end. Put your essay aside for awhile—even an hour would help—and come back to it with a fresh mind. Maybe then you will have a better idea for the conclusion.

Looking at Other Students' Writing

Look at Su-Wung Yu's essay on page 68 of Project 2. What did he do in his
conclusion? _____

_____

_____

_____

Look also at Michael Lim's essay on page 105 of Project 3. How did he end his
essay? _____

_____

_____

_____

Improving the Conclusion in Your Writing

Look at the essays that you have written so far in this course. How did you end
them? Choose one essay whose conclusion you are unhappy with, and revise
the ending or write a new one. Write as many drafts as necessary to get a conclusion
that you feel is ready for evaluation. When you finish, remember to clip together
the old essay and the new conclusion so your teacher and classmates can see the
improvement.

WRITING SKILLS: ACHIEVING COHERENCE

Using Cause-and-Effect Connectors

In the previous chapter you looked at how logical connectors help a reader to
follow your ideas, and you practiced using connectors to show difference. This
chapter will give you practice using cause-and-effect connectors, words and
phrases that show cause, effect, purpose, or condition.

Practice Using Cause-and-Effect Connectors

EXERCISE 1

The following sentences need cause and effect connectors to show how they are
related. Add the connector shown in parentheses and change or add any punctuation necessary.

1. Ms. Jamison, my first-grade teacher, was the person who taught me to read

    and to love books. I can never forget her. Every year on Teachers' Day I send

    her a card and tell her how important she has been in my life. (so)

2. In eighth grade we did exciting experiments in biology class. I became interested in medicine as a career. (such . . . that)

3. A few years ago I tried to help my sister with math. However, this attempt to teach was unsuccessful. I have never tried to teach anyone anything since then. (so . . . that)

4. I don't think I am a very good teacher. I will only teach someone something. The person asks me to do it. (since, if)

5. Whenever I teach someone something, I try to put myself in her place. I can anticipate what problems she will have and what she will need to have explained. (so that)

6. School should be an exciting place. Children will want to attend and not just come. Their parents or society forces them to. (such . . . that, because)

7. A good teacher needs to be patient. When students don't understand, she or he can explain again without getting angry and making the students feel stupid. (so that)

8. The worst teacher I ever had was my high-school gym teacher. He was a very good athlete himself. He thought everyone else should be too, and he laughed at students who weren't good at sports or gymnastics. A lot of students were embarrassed and hated to come to class. (because, as a result)

EXERCISE 2

The two passages that follow could be improved by adding cause and effect connectors to show the reason, result, purpose, or condition. Read them and add connectors to make the meaning clearer and the flow of ideas smoother. Change any punctuation as necessary.

1. Many students think history is a boring subject. They spend most of their time memorizing long lists of names and dates and causes of wars. They see nothing interesting in the material and no relevance to their own lives. But history itself is not boring; it is just the way it is taught that is boring. History could be taught as a good story—which it is. Students would find it much more fascinating.

2. In many parts of the world, university education is free or low cost. It is supported by the national or local government. In most such countries, how-

ever, there are only a small number of universities relative to the population. Competition for entrance is very keen and only a small number of students can be admitted each year. Most students have no opportunity to receive a college education.

In the United States, in contrast, there are many more universities relative to the size of the student body. A much larger proportion of the student population can attend college. But many universities are private institutions that receive no or only limited funds from the government and must charge high tuition fees to students who wish to attend. Many public universities and colleges have also increased their fees recently. The government has reduced its support for education. American students have more opportunity to receive a college education than students in other countries, but that education often costs far more.

Moving from One Idea to Another

> *Word carpentry is like any other carpentry: you must join your sentences smoothly.*
>
> *ANATOLE FRANCE*

Using logical connectors and ordering ideas logically are not the only ways to help your reader follow your thoughts. Fitting sentences together so that ideas flow smoothly is also important. The following paragraph is the introduction to an essay in which the writer compares high school to college. As you read it, think about whether or not she has prepared you for each new idea or helped you to follow her train of thought.

> ¹College is a very special place. ²Everybody has a dream that one day they can go to college and continue their education. ³There are some differences between high school and college. ⁴Most students say that they like college better than high school.

Each sentence in this paragraph contains the word *college*, so there is some relationship between them. Yet each sentence seems independent of the others. Sentence 2 has no obvious relation to sentence 1. Similarly, sentence 3 has no apparent relation to sentence 2. To a native English speaker the sentences do not follow one another smoothly.

In English, a well-written passage is not just a series of grammatically correct sentences lined up one after the other like telephone poles along a highway. Rather, a coherent piece of writing is like a jigsaw puzzle. The sentences must interlock; each fits into the others by relating back to what has come before and moving forward to introduce something new. English commonly gives old information at the beginning of a sentence and new information toward the end of a sentence. In the next sentence, the new information then becomes the old information and the sentence moves on to add new information. If we diagram this interlocking pattern, it looks like this:

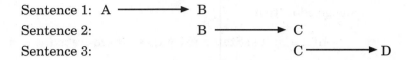

Sentence 1: A ⟶ B
Sentence 2:   B ⟶ C
Sentence 3:   C ⟶ D

The following paragraph is a revised version of the earlier one comparing high school to college. As you read it, think about how it is different from the original. What does the writer do to help you follow the ideas?

¹College is a very special place. ²It is where everyone dreams of going to continue their education. ³However, the educational system in college is very different from that of high school. ⁴Comparing the two, most students say that they like college better than high school.

The next example is a paragraph that a native English speaker would say lacks coherence because of the way in which the ideas are presented, but the problem is not as obvious as it is in the previous example. Here the writer discusses one of the reasons that she hates to write.

¹First, writing takes too much time. ²If I need to write an essay, I have to spend the whole day working on it even though it may only have three pages. ³I am the type of person who likes everything perfect. ⁴So when I write anything, I always try my best. ⁵I spend a long time thinking and trying hard to clearly give readers my ideas; and I carefully choose material to interest my readers. ⁶Also, I spend a lot of time checking my grammar and spelling and seeing if my organization, logic, and words are correct. ⁷Thus, whenever I must write something, I have no time to do other things. ⁸I have to give up part of my sleeping time when I must write while I have other work to do. ⁹I really dislike losing my rest time and that makes me hate writing even more.

Compare that paragraph to this more coherent version.

¹First, writing takes too much time. ²If I need to write an essay, I have to spend the whole day working on it even though it may only have three pages. ³The reason it takes me so long is that I am the type of person who likes everything perfect. ⁴So when I write anything, I always try my best. ⁵I spend a long time thinking and trying hard to clearly give readers my ideas; and I carefully choose material to interest my readers. ⁶Also, I spend a lot of time checking my grammar and spelling and seeing if my organization, logic, and words are correct. ⁷Thus, whenever I must write something, I have no time to do other things. ⁸If I have any other work to

do when I must write, I have to give up part of my sleeping time. ⁹I really dislike losing my rest time and that makes me hate writing even more.

What improvement is made by adding a clause to sentence 3? Think about what sentences 2 and 3 are talking about, what the topic or subject of each sentence is.   In sentence 2 the writer talks about her writing habits.   In sentence 3 she describes her character. What logical connection is there between these ideas? In the original paragraph, the relationship is not clear to the reader. In the revised paragraph, the added clause links sentence 3 to sentence 2 and allows the reader to follow the ideas more easily.

Next, compare the order of the clauses in sentence 8 in the original and revised paragraphs. Why is the new order better? Again think about the sentence topics. In sentences 7, 8, and 9, the writer discusses three subjects: having to write, doing other things, and losing sleep. If we label these ideas A, B, and C and diagram the sentences, we can see how the writer moves from one idea to the other.

Here are the sentences from the original paragraph.

⁷Whenever I must write something, I have no time to do other things. ⁸I have to give up part of my sleeping time when I must write while I have other work to do. ⁹ I really dislike losing my rest time and that makes me hate writing even more.

In this sequence of ideas, we find the order: ABCABC. Notice how far apart the alike letters are. The similar ideas are too separated.

Here are the sentences from the revised paragraph:

⁷Whenever I must write something, I have no time to do other things. ⁸If I have any other work to do when I must write, I have to give up part of my sleeping time. ⁹ I really dislike losing my rest time and that makes me hate writing even more.

In this sequence of ideas, we find the order ABBACC. The similar ideas are closer together. To a native English reader, this writing pattern flows more smoothly. It is easier to follow.

> Coherence is not a characteristic of individual sentences. Rather _coherence_ refers to how sentences fit together to form a paragraph and to how paragraphs fit together to form an essay.

Practice Moving from One Idea to Another

The passage that follows is the introduction and first body paragraph of a student's essay on the problems he encountered at college and his recommendations for solving them. Because some of the sentences do not fit well with what comes before or after them, the ideas do not flow smoothly. First, read the passage and underline sentences that don't fit well. Then rewrite the sentences so the passage flows more smoothly. (_Hint:_ there is one problem sentence in the first paragraph and two problem sentences in the second paragraph.)

Time really flies fast. My first semester at college is almost over. During the past three months, I have learned a lot and matured a lot. But unremitting problems have left me exhausted. A lot of problems unique to foreign students who cannot speak English well have especially bothered me.

First, I had serious problems when I chose my courses. Of course, I attended the advisement meetings before registration, but I didn't get the information I needed. All I was told about were the courses that were restricted. What courses I could take was never told to me by anyone. So I ran to the ESL office to get some advice. But the room was crowded, and I had to wait for more than thirty minutes in the line. Also, since my English was not very good, I had a difficult time understanding the advisor. There are many foreign students who suffer from a lack of information about choosing courses. Thus I think an information booth that explains what courses are available to foreign students and gives necessary information in a way that foreign students can understand should be provided in the registration area by the school.

Improving the Coherence of Your Writing

Look back at the essays you have written. Find one with a paragraph that you think could be improved by reorganizing the information or bridging the gaps between sentences. Do not change your meaning. Just make the ideas flow more smoothly by reordering the ideas or adding a word, a phrase, or a sentence to connect your ideas. When you have finished, clip the revised paragraph to the original essay.

SUGGESTED JOURNAL TOPICS

1. The Rockefeller Foundation has announced plans for an annual Best Teacher Award. It will be given to a teacher at any level: elementary school, high school, or college. However, before the program begins, the Foundation is asking students to help them develop a list of characteristics of a good teacher. Write a letter to the Foundation listing and defining the criteria you think they should use.

2. Oscar Wilde (1854–1900), a well-known Irish author, claimed, "Nothing that is worth knowing can be taught." Do you agree?

3. If I were teaching this course, this is what I would do.

4.

"THIS CLASS WILL STIMULATE YOUR IDEAS AND THOUGHTS. AND REMEMBER— NO TALKING."

Reprinted by permission of Jim Warren.

Can you learn without talking?

5. Write a letter to your favorite teacher.

6. Which is easier: being a teacher or being a student? Why?

7. "Teaching is . . ." Finish this thought at least six different ways. "Learning is . . ." Again, finish this thought at least six different ways.

8. Who should be paid more: teachers, lawyers, or garbage collectors?

9. It has been suggested that all teachers should occasionally spend a semester as a student again. What do you think of the idea?

10. What is your earliest memory of school?

11. James Baker, an American writer and professor, was interested in the question of what makes a real student. He examined this question in an essay in which he classified American college students into a number of different types. Here is part of his essay describing some of the categories he identifies. As you read the excerpt, notice how Baker entertains his readers—and makes his main point clearer—by using an exaggerated stereotype to define each category. Notice, too, how he makes this a playful essay by using informal language and descriptive details. Think about his types. Do any of them describe you? What kind of student are you?

° **people (verb):** inhabit, sit in

Has anyone else noticed that the very same students people° college classrooms year after year? Has anyone else found the same bodies, faces, personalities returning semester after semester? Forgive me for violating my students' individual "personhoods," but reality makes it so tempting to see them as types. Doubtless you will recognize at least some of them. They have twins . . . on your campus, too.

° **makes:** goes to, attends (informal)

° **mono:** short form of mononucleosis, an illness common among college students
° **shakes up:** bothers (informal)
° **esoteric:** understood by only a small number of people
° **obscure:** not well known
° **working up:** developing (informal)
° **give a nod to:** recognize
° **mundane:** ordinary

° **jock:** derogatory term for a man who is very interested in sports
° **liniment:** oily liquid rubbed into the skin to sooth sore muscles
° **Brut:** a brand of cologne for men
° **he-man-ism:** masculinity, maleness
° **obstacle course:** something that interferes with one's progress
° **hound:** hunting dog

° **cruising:** walking or driving around looking for something to do
° **Dairee-Freeze:** a chain of ice cream stores
° **despair:** hopelessness, discouragement

° **settling:** deciding
° **distressed:** disturbed, upset
° **dropout:** a person who leaves school without completing the program

There is the eternal Good Time Charlie (or Charlene), who makes° every party on and off the campus, . . . who misses every set of examinations because of "mono,"° who finally burns himself out physically and mentally by the age of 19 and drops out to go home and recuperate, and who returns at 20 after a long talk with Dad to major in accounting. . . .

There is the Egghead, the campus intellectual who shakes up° his fellow students—and even a professor or two—with references to esoteric° formulas and obscure° Bulgarian poets. . . .

There is the Performer—the music or theater major, the rock or folk singer—who spends all of his or her time working up° an act, who gives barely a nod° to mundane° subjects like history, sociology, or physics, who dreams only of the day he or she will be on stage full time, praised by critics, cheered by audiences. . . .

There is the Jock,° of course . . . smelling of liniment° and Brut,° with bulging calves and a blue-eyed twinkle, the subject of untold numbers of female fantasies, the walking personification of he-man-ism.° . . .

There is the Academic Gymnast—the guy or gal who sees college as an obstacle course,° as so many stumbling blocks in the way of a great career or a perfect marriage—who strains every moment to finish and be done with "this place" forever. . . .

There is the Medal Hound,° the student who comes to college not to learn or expand any intellectual horizons but simply to win honors—medals, cups, plates, ribbons, scrolls—who is here because this is the best place to win the most the fastest. . . .

There is the Worker Ant . . . who takes 21 hours [of class] a semester and works 49 hours a week at the local car wash, who sleeps only on Sundays and during classes. . . .

There is the Lost Soul, the sad kid who is in college only because teachers, parents and society . . . said so, who hasn't a career in mind or a dream to follow . . . , who heads home every Friday afternoon to spend the weekend cruising° the local Dairee-Freeze.° . . .

Then, finally, there is the Happy Child, who comes to college to find a husband or wife. . . .

All of which, I suppose, should make me throw up my hands in despair° and say that education, like youth and love, is wasted on the young. Not quite.

For there does come along, on occasion, that one of a hundred or so who is maybe at first a bit lost, certainly puzzled; who may well start out a Good Timer, an Egghead, a Performer, a Jock, a Medal Hound, a Gymnast, a Worker Ant; who may indeed have trouble settling° on a major, who will be distressed° by what sometimes passes for education, who might even be a temporary dropout;° but who has a vital capacity for growth and is able to fall in love with learning, who acquires a taste for intellectual pleasure, who becomes in the finest sense of the word a Student.

12. What is the difference between schooling and education?

13. Aristotle, the Greek philosopher, said, "The roots of education are bitter, but the fruit is sweet." What do you think he meant by that statement?

14. On a piece of scrap paper, write the heading *Thinking about School*. Below it make a list of at least fifteen words or phrases, positive or negative, that relate to school. Then arrange the words or phrases in the best sounding order, and write them one below the other on your journal page.

15. What subject did you hate the most in high school?

16. Think about the best teacher you ever had. Think about the best learning experience you ever had. Think about what you are learning now or would like to learn soon. And think about how you go about learning something. If you could design an educational system that would make all of these thoughts a reality, what would it be like?

17. Robert Fulghum, an American writer and educator, said: "In learning, don't ask for food, ask for farming lessons." What's the difference?

18.

Reprinted by permission of Harley Schwadron.

What do you think is the best way to measure what students have learned?

19. Sue Hubbell, a beekeeper in the Ozark Mountains of southern Missouri wrote, "Over the past twelve years I have learned that a tree needs space to grow, that coyotes sing down by the creek in January, that I can drive a nail into oak only when it is green, that bees know more about making honey than I do, that love can become sadness, and that there are more questions than answers." What have you learned over the past twelve years?

ADDITIONAL WRITING TOPICS

1. The excerpt from James Baker's article on pages 159–60 groups students into categories. Teachers, too, can be grouped in many ways: by age, sex, subject they teach, and so on. They can also be categorized by their qualities or characteristics. Think about all the teachers you have had and decide what categories you could put them in. Use examples to illustrate each category.

2. Most foreigners who enroll in school in this country say that the way of teaching and learning here is very different from their own country. Do you think that's true? Compare the teaching style and classroom atmosphere you have found here to those you experienced in your native country.

3. Most American university students say they prefer college to high school. What do you think? Think back to your high school days and compare them to your experiences at this institution. Which do you prefer and why?

4. Reread the essay by Tama Janowitz on pages 135–36. What kind of teachers sparked her interest in learning particular subjects? What do you want to study and what got you interested in this subject?

5. Everyone talks about good and bad teachers; less often do people talk about good and bad students. Describe an ideal student, and discuss the extent to which you approach this ideal.

ADDITIONAL READINGS

Mortimer J. Adler. "Schooling Is Not Education." *The New York Times*. Reprinted in *The College Writer's Reader*, pp. 36–37. Edited by William Vesterman. New York: McGraw-Hill 1988.

Caroline Bird. "Where College Fails Us." *Signature Magazine* 1975. Diners' Club, Inc. Reprinted in *A Writer's Reader*, 6th ed. Edited by Donald Hall and D. L. Emblem. New York: HarperCollins 1991.

Judith Ortiz Cofer. "Primary Lessons" and "One More Lesson." *Silent Dancing: A Partial Remembrance of a Puerto Rican Childhood*. pp. 51–58, 61–66. Houston: Arte Publico Press 1990.

Sydney J. Harris. "What True Education Should Do." *The Chicago Sun Times* 1989. Reprinted in *Guidelines: A Cross-Cultural Reading / Writing Text* by Ruth Spack. pp. 9–10. New York: St. Martin's Press 1990.

Richard Rodriguez. "The Achievement of Desire." *Hunger of Memory*, Chapter 2. Boston: David R. Godine 1982. Parts of this chapter are also reprinted in *The Dolphin Reader* (Edited by Douglas Hurt. NY: Houghton-Mifflin 1986) and *Life Studies: A Thematic Reader*, 3rd ed. (Edited by David Cavitch. New York: St. Martin's Press 1989).

PROJECT

5

CHOOSING A CAREER

This final project will give you the chance to use all the writing strategies you have practiced during the semester. It will give you the opportunity to show what you have learned about the process of writing and how well you are able to improve your writing.

In this project you will

- brainstorm for ideas to write about and outline (before you begin to write).
- draft your essay and then revise it to improve the unity, development, and coherence of your ideas.
- develop an appropriate introduction and conclusion.
- edit your essay to make it grammatically correct.
- continue to write in your journal.

GETTING IDEAS

Starting to Think about the Topic of This Project

For this project you are going to think about careers and choices. In your native country, can people freely choose their careers? If not, who or what limits their choices? Using the space provided below, brainstorm for ten minutes on "Choosing a Career in My Country." Use any of the brainstorming methods you have practiced: listing, free-writing, asking wh– questions, or clustering.

_____

_____

_____

_____

_____

_____

_____

_____

_____

_____

_____

_____

_____

_____

_____

_____

_____

_____

Getting Ideas through Reading

1.   Have you decided what career you will follow? How old were you when that decision was made?

2.   Do you think you will be economically more or less successful than your parents?

3.   At a university, should students take courses that will directly help them get a job, or should they study whatever interests them and not worry about getting a job until after graduation?

Student Michael Finkel wrote the following article, "Undecided—and Proud of It," about his career plans. At the time, he was a senior at the Wharton School of the University of Pennsylvania. The Wharton School is one of the best-known business schools in the United States.

° **Wall Street:** a New York street famous for banking and finance businesses

° **blueprint:** plan

° **picket fence:** fence made of upright, pointed pieces of wood
° **spanking-new:** very new
° **heck:** mild curse (considered more polite than saying "Hell.")
° **resume:** written summary of your educational and professional life (given to employers when you want a job)
° **launch:** start
° **drives:** pushes
° **emulate:** copy

° **definitive:** fully developed

° **firms:** businesses
° **have a jump on:** be ahead of or in advance of
° **zealous:** enthusiastic
° **recruiter:** person who finds new employees

° **gobs:** large amount

"Go to Wall Street,"° my classmates said.
"Go to Wall Street," my professor advised.
"Go to Wall Street," my father threatened.

Whenever I tell people about my career indecisiveness, their answer is always the same: Get a blueprint° for life and get one fast. Perhaps I'm simply too immature, but I think 20 is far too young to set my life in stone.

Nobody mentioned any award for being the first to have a white picket fence,° 2.4 screaming kids and a spanking-new° Ford station wagon.

What's wrong with uncertainty, with exploring multiple options in multiple fields? What's wrong with writing, "Heck,° I don't know" under the "objective" section of my resume?°

Parents, professors, recruiters, and even other students seem to think there's a lot wrong with it. And they are all pressuring me to launch° a career prematurely.

My sociology professor warns that my generation will be the first in American history not to be more successful than our parents' generation. This depressing thought drives° college students to think of success as something that must be achieved at all costs as soon as possible.

My father wants me to emulate° his success: every family wants its children to improve the family fortune. I feel that desire myself, but I realize I don't need to do it by age 25.

This pressure to do better, to compete with the achievements of our parents in a rapidly changing world, has forced my generation to pursue definitive,° lifelong career paths at far too young an age. Many of my friends who have graduated in recent years are already miserably unhappy.

My professors encourage such pre-professionalism. In upper level finance classes, the discussion is extremely career-oriented. "Learn to do this and you'll be paid more" is the theme of many a lecture. Never is there any talk of actually enjoying the exercise.

Nationwide, universities are finally taking steps in the right direction by re-emphasizing the study of liberal arts and a return to the classics. If only job recruiters for Wall Street firms° would do the same.

"Get your M.B.A. as soon as possible and you'll have a jump on° the competition," said one overly zealous° recruiter° from Goldman Sachs. Learning for learning's sake was completely forgotten: Goldman Sachs refused to interview anybody without a high grade-point average, regardless of the courses composing that average.

In other interviews, it is expected that you know exactly what you want to do or you won't be hired. "Finance?" they say, "What kind of finance?"

A recruiter at Dean Witter Reynolds said investment banking demands 80 to 100 hours of work per week. I don't see how anyone will ever find time to enjoy the gobs° of money they'll be making.

The worst news came from a partner at Salomon Brothers. He told me no one was happy there, and if they said they were, they're lying. He said you come in here, make a lot of money, and leave as fast as you can.

° **alumni:** graduates

Two recent Wharton alumni,° scarcely two years older than I, spoke at Donaldson, Lufkin & Jenrette's presentation. Their jokes about not having a life outside the office were only partially in jest.°

° **in jest:** in fun
° **charade:** game in which players pretend to be someone or something else

Yet, students can't wait to play their corporate charade.° They don° ties and jackets and tote° briefcases to class.

° **don:** put on
° **tote:** carry
° **obsessed:** mentally fixed on just one thought
° **iota:** very small amount
° **implore:** beg; ask with great feeling

It is not just business students who are obsessed° with their careers. The five other people who live in my house are not undergraduate business majors, but all five plan to attend graduate school next year. How is it possible that, without one iota° of real work experience, these people are willing to commit themselves to years of intensive study in one narrow field?

Mom, dad, grandpa, recruiters, professors, fellow students: I implore° you to leave me alone.

° **toiling:** working very hard

Now is my chance to explore, to spend time pursuing interests simply because they make me happy and not because they fill my wallet. I don't want to waste my youth toiling° at a miserable job. I want to make the right decisions about my future.

Who knows, I may even end up on Wall Street.

Getting More Ideas through Discussion

Now you will have an opportunity to get more ideas about the topic of this project by talking to your classmates. Remember that it is important not only to listen to each other but also to question each other's thoughts and opinions. If you do not understand what someone says, ask for clarification. Maybe the person has not fully thought out the idea and needs encouragement to explore it.

Discussion Questions

Look at the following list of occupations before you read each question.

lawyer	cleric	sales clerk (clothing store)
college professor	politician	computer programmer
accountant	plumber	auto mechanic
secretary	doctor	teacher (high school)

1. Working by yourself, think about the *status* of each of these professions. *In your opinion,* which is the most respected or prestigious occupation? Which is the least respected? In the following chart, list the occupations in their order of status, starting with the one you think has the highest status (most respected) and ending with the one you consider has the lowest status (least respected).

After you finish your own list, ask the other members of your group for their lists and add them to your chart.

My List	(name 1)	(name 2)	(name 3)
highest status	_____	_____	_____
_____	_____	_____	_____
_____	_____	_____	_____
_____	_____	_____	_____
_____	_____	_____	_____
_____	_____	_____	_____
_____	_____	_____	_____
_____	_____	_____	_____
_____	_____	_____	_____
_____	_____	_____	_____
_____	_____	_____	_____
_____	_____	_____	_____

lowest status

2.   Working by yourself again, think about the *personal satisfaction* that each of these professions can provide. Which occupation do you think would give *you* the most pleasure? Which do you feel would give *you* the least sense of fulfillment? In the following chart list the occupations starting with the one you would find most satisfying and moving to the one you would find least satisfying. When you finish, read your list aloud to the members of your group. Are your lists similar or very different?

most satisfying

_____

_____

_____

_____

_____

_____

_____

_____

_____

least satisfying

3.   Now think about the potential *income* of these professions in this country. How much money do you think someone could earn in each of these occupations? Discuss this question as a group and in the following chart list the occupations in order from the highest income to the lowest income.

highest income

_____

_____

_____

_____

_____

_____

_____

_____

_____

_____

lowest income

4.   Finally, think about how questions 1 and 3 are connected. Do you see any relation between the amount of respect (status) people give to a particular occupation and the amount of money (income) someone can earn in that occupation? In the space below, free-write about this topic for ten minutes. When you finish, read your free-writing aloud to the rest of your group.

_____

_____

_____

_____

_____

_____

_____

_____

_____

_____

_____

_____

_____

_____

_____

_____

_____

_____

_____

_____

_____

_____

_____

_____

_____

_____

_____

ESSAY TOPICS FOR PROJECT 5

Now that you have some ideas on the subject of this project, it is time to write. Choose one of the following essay topics about choosing a career.

1. People choose a career for many different reasons. What are the various factors that most people take into account in choosing a career or profession? Which of these factors is or was most important to you?

2. Family pressure and cultural traditions can play important roles in career decisions. How important are these factors in your native country? To what extent have they influenced your choice of a career?

PREWRITING

Brainstorming

Brainstorm for ten minutes on your topic. Choose whichever technique you prefer: listing, free-writing, asking wh– questions, or clustering. Use a clean sheet of paper for your brainstorming, and leave lots of space so you can expand your ideas. Don't worry about how correct your English is or how messy the page looks. Focus on exploring your thoughts. Include any facts, examples, or explanations you could use to develop each point.

If you have any ideas for an introduction, take a separate piece of paper, write the heading *Introduction* and jot down your ideas. If you can't think of an interesting way to start, don't waste time worrying about it. You can begin writing your first draft with any sentence that comes to mind or you can begin with the body and go back to the introduction later.

If you have any ideas for a conclusion, write *Conclusion* on another piece of paper and note down your ideas. If not, don't spend time worrying; some ideas will probably come to you as you write your essay.

Outlining

If you find outlining useful, make an outline of your essay. Since writing is a process of discovering what you want to say, it is not always possible to outline your entire essay in advance. But outlining part of it before you write can help you focus on your main idea and ensure that it answers the question in the assignment, state your supporting ideas more clearly and judge their relevance, develop your ideas more fully, and plan the organization of your essay.

WRITING THE FIRST DRAFT

Now you are ready to write your first draft. If you made an outline, use it as a guide as you write your essay. If you did not make an outline, keep referring to your brainstorming as a source of ideas. Concentrate on getting your thoughts down on paper as clearly and as fully as you can. If you run out of ideas at any point, try brainstorming again. Remember to double space so you have room to add ideas if you want to and so you can revise directly on the draft. Your draft does not have to be beautiful, just readable.

When you have finished, read your essay from beginning to end. If possible, read it aloud. Is there any part that does not sound right to you? Is there any part you would like to change? Remember that Draft One is a work in progress. Keep writing and rewriting until you are told to stop.

REVISING YOUR DRAFT

In this last project you are going to try being your own critical reader. Although it is usually better to have someone else judge how successfully you have communicated, sometimes it is not possible. So you have to be objective about your own writing. Throughout the semester you have practiced responding to your classmates' essays. Now put on your reading hat and look at your own essay through a reader's eyes.

Outlining

In Project 4, as part of responding to a classmate's essay, you outlined the draft to help you see exactly what was said and how the ideas were organized. Many writers find it useful to outline their own first draft at this point for the same reasons. They say it helps them see their work as a reader would see it. If you think outlining would be helpful to you, make an outline now of your first draft.

Revision Questions

The following guide will help you think critically about your own writing. After you have considered each question, put a check (✔) after it.

1. Consider your *purpose, audience,* and *main idea.* Ask yourself:

   What am I trying to do in this essay and who are my readers?_____

   Do I state my main idea as directly and clearly as I can?_____

   Do I answer the question(s) in the assignment?_____

2. Think about the *development, unity,* and *coherence* of your essay as a whole. Ask yourself:

   Do I write enough to explain my main idea? What additional supporting ideas could I add to make sure that my readers understand my main idea?_____

   Is every supporting paragraph directly and closely related to my main idea? Are any paragraphs irrelevant?_____

   Is it clear how each supporting paragraph relates to the main idea or have I left it to the reader to guess the connection?_____

   Is this the best order for my paragraphs?_____

3. Think about the d*evelopment, unity,* and *coherence* of each supporting paragraph. Ask yourself:

   Is the paragraph sufficiently developed? Do I need to expand any of my thoughts so my readers will understand them?_____

   Is all the information in the paragraph directly and closely related to the point of the paragraph? Do I wander away from the point anywhere? Or do I fail to show the relevance of any idea?_____

   Do my ideas flow smoothly from sentence to sentence?_____

   Should I rearrange the order of any phrases or clauses?_____

   Are the logical connections between the ideas clear? _____

   Have I left any big gaps between ideas so that readers have to guess the connection?_____

4. Look at the *introduction*. Ask yourself:

Does it inform the reader about the topic?_____

Does it state or suggest the main idea of the essay?_____

Does it try to interest the reader?_____

Is it sufficiently developed and do the ideas flow smoothly?_____

5. Examine the *conclusion*. Ask yourself:

Does it give the reader the idea that the essay is ending?_____

Does it take the reader back to the main idea?_____

Is it interesting?_____

As you did for earlier projects, use Draft One as a base for writing Draft Two. Cross out words and sentences and rewrite them in the space above or in the margins. Use arrows to add material or move it to another place. Write new sections or paragraphs on a separate sheet and use letters or numbers to show where they should be added, or staple or tape them into place. If you are really revising, your draft will look messy. But don't worry; at this point, only *you* have to be able to read it.

Keep going back to the beginning of your draft and rereading the whole essay so that you remember what you are writing about and can see how the parts of the essay fit together. If possible, read your essay aloud. Listening to the sound of your writing can help you find ideas that don't relate logically, sentences that don't move smoothly, words that have been left out, and vocabulary that has been repeated.

When you think you have finished rewriting, look again at the guide questions. Are you more satisfied with your answers? If not, keep working.

When you have rewritten as much as you feel you can, make a list of your revisions as you did for previous projects.

Then decide whether your draft is still readable or you need to make a clean copy. If *you* can read and follow your revisions, a clean draft is not necessary. However, if your draft has become illegible even to you, neatly copy out Draft Two. Remember to double-space and write on one side of the page only.

EDITING

The final step in the writing process is to edit your essay. Use the Editing Checklist on page 175 as a guide. Remember to edit with a different color pen or pencil so you can see what you have changed.

Keep in mind how important careful editing is. If you can eliminate the kinds of errors listed on the Editing Checklist, you can significantly improve your essay. Sloppy editing—or no editing at all—will lead your readers to think that you don't know the grammar or that you don't care what they think about your writing. Give them the best impression of your writing that you can.

When you finish editing, write out a clean, final draft of your essay. Then clip together all the parts of the project, and hand them in to your teacher.

Editing Checklist 5

Draft checked by _____

You can successfully find many grammatical errors if you look for one kind of error at a time. Read your essay carefully several times, each time looking for and correcting *one* kind of error on the list below. As you finish checking for each type of error, place a check (✔) next to it on the list below.

_____ 1. Basic sentence components

Missing or repeated subject

Missing verb

Missing or repeated object /complement

_____ 2. Verbs

Wrong verb tense

Wrong verb form

_____ 3. Agreement

No subject-verb agreement

No agreement between a noun and its antecedent

_____ 4. Sentence boundaries

Fragments

Run-ons and comma splices

_____ 5. Pronouns

_____ 6. Punctuation

_____ 7. Spelling (*Hint*: To check spelling, read each line of words from right to left. This helps you see each word individually.)

Teacher's comments: _____

_____

_____

_____

_____

When you finish editing, attach this sheet to your draft.

SUGGESTED JOURNAL TOPICS

1.   The American writer Christopher Morley (1890–1957) said, "There is only one success—to be able to spend your life in your own way." What is your way?

2.   An obituary is a notice in a newspaper announcing the death of someone. In addition to giving the place and date of death, it discusses the person's life, career, and accomplishments. Pretend it is the year 2060 and you have just died. Write your own obituary.

3.   Bob Black, the author of a book titled *The Abolition of Work and Other Essays*, said, "You are what you do. If you do boring, stupid, monotonous work, chances are you'll end up boring, stupid, and monotonous." Do you think that's true?

4.   What career(s) would you *not* choose and why?

5.   Your parents very strongly want you to major in a particular subject (for example, computer science or accounting), but you decide you want to study a very different subject (for example, English literature or history). Write a letter to your parents explaining your choice.

6.   Today is Tuesday, November 7, 2010. Where are you and what are you doing?

7.   Many American teenagers work at part-time jobs to earn money for clothes, movies, a car, or their education. In the following paragraph, one young man describes his money-making activities.

° **hustling:** energetically working and looking for customers
° **squirreling:** hiding
° **devising:** thinking of
° **scheme:** plan
° **capitalize on:** take advantage of

> Making money has always been a passion of mine. At the age of 12, I was a hustling° newspaper boy and baby sitter, squirreling° away dollar bills in a small red plastic safe that I hid behind my socks. While my brother was out playing basketball, I was devising° plans to build my fortune. I cut lawns, delivered pizza, worked in a ware-house and as a security guard. I even had a scheme° in college to capitalize on° student birth control and sell condoms by mail order.

Have you ever worked for money during vacations, after school, or on week-ends? What did you do and what did you do with the money?

8.   Describe your idea of the *perfect job*.

9.   In an article called "Workers of the World, Relax," Bob Black wrote "No one should ever work. Work is the source of nearly all the misery in the world. Almost all evil you'd care to name comes from working or from living in a world designed for work. In order to stop suffering, we have to stop working." Do you agree?

10. What do the words *work* and *job* mean? What's the difference between them? What words do you have in your native language to express these ideas?

11.

" I'D LIKE TO PURSUE A CAREER WHERE I CAN BENEFIT
MANKIND BUT STILL HAVE WEEKENDS OFF. "

©1993 Frank Cotham

Write the rest of the dialogue between the student and the guidance counselor.

12. "If people are highly successful in their professions they lose their senses. They have no time to look at pictures. Sound goes. They have no time to listen to music. Speech goes. They have no time for conversation. They lose their sense of proportion—the relations between one thing and another. Humanity goes. . . ." (Virginia Woolf) Do you think that is true?

13. You have just won one million dollars in the lottery. Will you look for a job after you graduate, or will you just live off your winnings?

14. Marilyn Monroe said, "I don't want to make money. I just want to be wonderful." Which do you prefer?

ADDITIONAL READINGS

Rhoda Gillinsky. "How Will We Find the Philosophers in a World of Lawyers and Doctors?" *The Chronicle of Higher Education* XXIII (24): 25, 1982.

Marshall Glickman. "Money and Freedom." *The New York Times Magazine*, p. 62. April 26, 1987.

Daniel Meier. "One Man's Kids." *The New York Times Magazine*. 1987. Reprinted in *Life Studies: A Thematic Reader*, 3rd ed. Edited by David Cavitch. New York: St. Martin's Press 1989.

Beverly Stephen. "A Career for the '90s: Teaching Is Back!" *Woman's Day* 54 (15): 72–74, Nov. 5, 1991.

Gloria Steinem. "The Importance of Work." *Outrageous Acts and Everyday Rebellions*. Holt, Rinehart & Winston 1983. Reprinted in *The Bedford Reader*, 2nd ed. Edited by X. J. Kennedy and Dorothy M. Kennedy. New York: St. Martin's Press 1985.

GRAMMAR

PARTS OF THE SENTENCE

In English, all written sentences have two basic parts: a *subject* (s) and a *verb* (v). The *subject* tells who or what the sentence is about. The *verb* tells what the subject is or does.

```
          S            V
The little boy    laughed.
          S            V
All the students    were dancing.
```

> A group of words containing a subject and verb is called a *clause*. To be grammatically complete, a sentence must always have at least one clause.

Many sentences have a third part: an *object* (o) or *complement* (c).

```
      S          V           O
My neighbor    bought    a new car.
      S          V           O
Susanna      is studying    English.
          S            V        C
The grammar exam      seemed    easy.
```

In most English sentences, the subject comes first, the verb next, and the object or complement last. The usual order of the parts is: S-V-O or C.

Most sentences have a fourth part: a *modifier* (MOD). Modifiers tell us more about the subject, the verb, or the object. A modifier can be one word or a group of words and can come at many places in the sentence.

```
          S            V        MOD
The little boy    laughed    at the clown.
    MOD          S           V         O
Last week    my neighbor    bought    a new car.
    S          MOD              V         MOD       MOD
Some   of the students    were sitting    quietly    on the floor.
```

To correct many of your sentence errors, you must be able to identify the parts of a sentence.

How to Find the Subject

To find the subject of a sentence, look for the words that tell you *what* or *who* the sentence is about.

what?
The most popular books are listed on page two.

who?
My older brother got married two years ago.

The most important word in the subject is the *simple subject*. In the previous examples, *books* and *brother* are the simple subjects.

Important Points to Remember about Subjects

1. The simple subject is always a noun or a word or words equivalent to a noun. In these examples, the simple subject is a noun.

   Her *friends* agreed to help organize the party.

   April *showers* bring May flowers.

   In these examples, the simple subject is a noun equivalent.

PRONOUN	*She* promised to call this evening. *They* never arrive on time.
INFINITIVE	*To fail* is really embarrassing.
GERUND	*Vacuuming* is the most boring household chore.
CLAUSE	*That she died so young* was a tragedy.

2. The subject can never be omitted from the sentence. Even pronoun subjects cannot be left out (as they can in some other languages).

WRONG	*Is a lovely day today. *Are no clouds in the sky.
RIGHT	*It* is a lovely day today. *There* are no clouds in the sky.

3. There can be more than one subject.

   Swimming and *bicycling* are my favorite sports.
   The debating *team* and the computer *club* meet on Tuesdays.

   But the same subject cannot be repeated.

WRONG	*My older *sister she* came to visit me. *The *city* I come from in Japan *it* is very interesting.
RIGHT	My older *sister* came to visit me. The *city* I come from in Japan is very interesting.

4. The simple subject is never found within a prepositional phrase. A

prepositional phrase is a group of words that begins with a preposition: for example, *at, to, of, in, before, toward, during*.

<pre>
         S   prep phrase   prep phrase
The chair <i>in the middle</i>   <i>of the row</i> is broken.

         S   prep phrase   prep phrase
Standing <i>under a tree</i>   <i>during a storm</i>   is dangerous.
</pre>

WRONG   *In my *high school* had many student clubs.
               *During my history *class* was very interesting.

RIGHT   My *high school* had many student clubs.

               My history *class* was very interesting.

Practice Finding Subjects

Underline the simple subjects in the sentences that follow. Check your answers at the bottom of the page.

1. The first time in my life that I thought about a career was in high school.

2. Every wall and every ceiling in the house was painted a different color.

3. After winning first place in the contest, the five members of the team posed for pictures with their parents.

4. Although there was no hint of rain, the school administrators and teachers decided to hold the sports carnival inside.

How to Find the Verb

1. To find the verb in a sentence look for the word that tells you what the subject does or did.

   > My friend's cat died last week.
   > What did the cat do? It *died*.

   > After much thought, she decided to look for another cat.
   > What did she do? She *decided*.

2. Put a pronoun in front of the word that you think is a verb. If the result is grammatically correct, the word is a verb. Look at the sentence:

   An old man sitting next to the window was laughing quietly.

In this sentence, *sitting* looks like a verb. But because you cannot say *he sitting*, *sitting* is not a verb here. An *-ing* verb must always have an *auxiliary* (a helping verb) to indicate tense. Now look at *was laughing*. Because you can say *he was laughing, was laughing* is a verb.

Answers: 1. time, I   2. wall and ceiling   3. members   4. there, administrators and teachers

3. Look for the word that changes to show tense.

> The trip from New York to the Mexican border takes three days by car. Yesterday we *drove* from New York to Ohio. Today we*'re driving* from Ohio to Arkansas. Tomorrow we*'ll arrive* at the Mexican border.

Important Points to Remember about Verbs

1. Many verbs have several parts. The whole verb is called a *verb phrase*.

> By 1998, Laura *will have graduated* from college.

2. A sentence can have more than one verb describing one subject.

> Our cat *gets up, eats* breakfast, and *goes* back to sleep.

> The new president *hugged* his wife and *kissed* his daughter.

3. An infinitive is never the verb of a sentence.

> I *want* to come to see you.

In this example, *to come* and *to see* are not verbs.

However, if *to* is part of the auxiliary as in *have to, going to,* or *ought to,* then *to* is part of the verb phrase.

> I *have to show* you something. Then I *am going to leave.*

In these examples, *have to show* and *am going to leave* are verbs.

Practice Finding Verbs

Double underline each verb in the sentences below. Check your answers at the bottom of the page.

1. Last Sunday, I locked my door, took my phone off the hook, and spent the whole day working on my English homework.

2. I was born in Argentina, spent the first ten years of my life in Brazil, and then came to live in Canada.

3. My parents were going to come to visit me this summer, but they decided to postpone their trip until November.

How to Find the Object

To find the object of a verb in a sentence, look for the word that completes the meaning of the verb. (Usually the object follows the verb.) Objects, like subjects,

Answers: 1. locked, took, spent 2. was, spent, came 3. were going to come, decided

give information about *what* or *who*. Thus, to find the object, you can use the subject and verb in a question with *what* or *who*.

Katrina loves Italian food.

What does Katrina love? (or Katrina loves *what*?)   *Italian food*

Katrina wants to go home.

What does Katrina want? (or *Katrina* wants *what*?)   *to go home*

Katrina said that she was tired.

What did Katrina say? (or Katrina said *what*?)   *that she was tired*

Verbs that must always have an object are called *transitive* and are marked *vt* in the dictionary.

Important Points to Remember about Objects

1. Not every sentence has an object. Whether or not the sentence has an object depends on the verb used. Some verbs never take an object. They are called *intransitive* and are marked *vi* in the dictionary. They can be followed by information about *where*, *when*, *why*, or *how*, but never *what* or *who*.

S	V	MOD	MOD	S	V	MOD
We	arrived	at the movie	early.	We	had to wait	in line.
		where?	when?			where?

    Many verbs can be either transitive or intransitive depending on whether or not they are followed by an object.

S	V	O	
He	usually speaks	*English*	at home.

S	V	MOD	MOD
She	spoke	*without notes*	*for two hours.*

2. An object is always a noun or noun-equivalent (pronoun, infinitive, gerund, or clause). Any word or group of words that can be a subject can be an object.

3. There can be two different objects (*who* and *what*) of a verb.

S	V	O	O
I	lent	*him*	*fifteen dollars.*
		who?	what?

S	V	O	O	
He	gave	*me*	*a ride*	home.
		who?	what?	

4. Objects do not only follow verbs; they also follow prepositions.

    We sat in the *kitchen* and talked about *politics.*
    what?   what?

How to Find the Complement

In some cases, the word that completes the meaning of the verb renames or describes the subject of the sentence. This kind of word is called a *complement* (not an object). The complement can be a noun, or it can be an adjective or adverb.

S   V   C   S   V   C

Larry is a *teenager* now. He is growing *taller* every day.

S   V   C   S   V   C

My sister felt *sick* yesterday, but today she seems *fine*.

Verbs that are followed by a complement are called *linking* verbs. The verb *be,* when used as a main verb, is always a linking verb. Other common linking verbs are: *appear, feel, become, grow, seem, look, remain, smell, sound,* and *taste*.

Practice Finding Objects and Complements

Go back to the verb-finding exercise on page 182. Look for the objects and complements and draw a wavy line under each one. Check your answers at the bottom of this page.

Practice Finding Basic Sentence Parts

The following paragraph comes from Laura Waterbury's essay about being an atheist that you read in Project 1. Read the passage and mark the simple subjects with a single underline, the verbs with a double underline, and the objects or complements with a wavy line. If the object or complement is a clause, mark it with brackets. Sentences 1 and 8 are done for you as examples.

¹I never thought about my atheism, or even considered it out of the ordinary until I was eight. ²I had thought that not believing in God was common and widely accepted; it was like my belief that everyone had a passport just because I had always had one. ³I remember I was sitting in class. ⁴It was the fourth grade, the first of the two years that I spent living in Ecuador. ⁵I was surrounded by a group of girls, all of whom accompanied their parents to church every Sunday. ⁶They were all talking about God and, as I usually do, I opened my big mouth. ⁷They couldn't understand the concept of God not existing, nor do I think they had ever met anyone who believed that. ⁸I remember [what they told me].⁹They said: "Well, if you don't believe in God, then you're going to go to hell." ¹⁰That would have scared any child right into God's hands, including me, but my best friend Patricia piped up and saved me from doubting my doubt. ¹¹She said, "But if she doesn't believe in hell, how can she go there?" ¹²And I thought to myself, "Yeah, that's right." ¹³Now when I look back to that time, I realize what an intelligent thing she said, especially for an eight year old.

Practice Correcting Errors in Basic Sentence Parts

Students often have problems with the subject, the verb, the object, or the complement of their sentences. However, if you can identify the basic sentence parts, you can begin to correct some of your errors. Each of the following passages contains errors in subject, verb, object, or complement. Single underline the simple subject, double underline the verb, and put a wavy line under and/or brackets around the object or complement. As you do this look for mistakes and correct them.

Example

The worst <u>thing</u> about me _^ is [<u>I</u> <u>am</u> impatient.]

1. My first bad characteristic is laziness. I never like to work. Maybe is the environment that I work in. Sometimes I think I should change my job. But I always tell myself to make the best of what I have. Every time I end up saying, "There always next time."

2. My best quality is I like help other people who have problems. For example, I like give clothes to children don't have any.

3. I often too hurried. I drive too fast and I eat too fast. Therefore make many mistakes in my life.

4. My worst characteristic is very impatient. I don't like to wait. For example, when my brother tells me that will be back in five minutes and should wait for him and doesn't come back, I get angry.

5. Another negative characteristic I afraid to talk to people. When I am with a lot of people or when the teacher asks me something, even if I know the answer, I cannot talk. I too shy.

6. My other good characteristic is helping other people. I cannot just stand by and watch when friends in trouble. I have to go to them and try to help them.

7. Sometimes I get into a bad mood and think that I alone and I am the worst person in the world. At that moment, I try to think of my positive characteristics so can feel better about myself.

FORM AND MEANING OF VERB TENSES

The tense of a verb tells when an action occurs in time—past, present, or future—and how the action is related to that time:

simple—occuring at that time
perfect—before that time
progressive—continuing at the time

Simple Forms

Simple forms express actions that occur at the point of time indicated.

Simple Present

I/you/we/they	+ base form
he/she/it	+ base form + *-s*

The simple present is used for general truths, scientific facts, and habitual or repeated actions in the present.

Jean *loves* sports. She *swims* every day and *plays* basketball on the weekend. I *am* just the opposite. I *hate* physical activity even though I *know* it *is* good for my health.

Simple Past

subject + past form
(verb+ *-ed*)

The simple past is used for specific events, general truths, and habitual or repeated actions in the past.

Last night I *cooked* dinner and *did* the dishes; I *worked* on this book; I *talked* to friends on the phone; and I *watched* an hour of TV. I *did*n't *go* to bed until after midnight.

Simple Future

English does not have just one simple future form. The simple future can be expressed several ways.

SIMPLE FUTURE using WILL

subject + will + base form

The simple future with *will* is used for promises and predictions (telling events or actions that are certain to occur in the future).

The weather report says that tomorrow *will be* hot and sunny so I *will pick* you up at nine and we *will go* to the beach.

SIMPLE FUTURE using BE GOING TO

> subject + am/is/are going to
> + base form

The simple future with *be going to* is used for intentions or plans and less formal predictions.

My friend's daughter *is going to major* in French at college, so she *is going to spend* the summer in Paris living with a French family.

The simple future can also be expressed using the present progressive tense and the simple future tense.

The present progressive tense is used for definite plans in the near future.

Ron *is flying* to Boston tomorrow. He *is running* in the Boston Marathon next Sunday.

The simple present tense is used for actions in the future that are fixed in time.

Thank you for shopping at Macy's. Our store *opens* again tomorrow at ten o'clock.

Perfect Forms

Perfect forms express actions that occur before another time or action.

PRESENT PERFECT

> subject + has/have + participle
>
> (participle = regular verb + *-ed*)
>
> (participle = 3rd form
> of irregular verbs)

I *have decided* what courses I want to take next semester, but I *haven't registered* for them yet.

The present perfect is used for actions that occurred in the past but are important or relevant now, or actions that began in the past and are still true now.

PAST PERFECT

> subject + had + participle
>
> (participle = regular verb + *-ed*)
>
> (participle = 3rd form
> of irregular verbs)

After we glued all the parts of the plane together, we realized we *had attached* the wings upside down. We also *had forgotten* to paint the inside of the cockpit.

The past perfect is used for past actions that occurred before another past action or time.

FUTURE PERFECT

subject+ will have + participle

(participle = regular verb + -*ed*)

(participle = 3rd form
of irregular verbs)

The future perfect is used for future actions that will occur before another future action or time.

Five years from now, most of you *will have forgotten* these grammar rules.

Progressive Forms

The progressive forms express repeated, continuing, or incomplete actions.

PRESENT PROGRESSIVE

subject+ am/is/are + verb + -*ing*

The present progressive is used for actions that are now in progress, unfinished, or for repeated actions.

Outside my window right now, dogs *are barking*, car horns *are blaring*, and a neighbor *is playing* loud music on his stereo.

PAST PROGRESSIVE

subject+ was/were + verb + -*ing*

The past progressive is used for unfinished or interrupted past actions, or repeated actions or actions of long duration in the past.

When we arrived, all the children *were swimming* in the pond.

The weather was so hot that people *were swimming* in the pond day and night.

FUTURE PROGRESSIVE

subject+ will be + verb + -*ing*

The future progressive is used for continuing or unfinished future actions.

The painters *will be working* upstairs all day tomorrow and the next day.

Perfect-Progressive Forms

The perfect-progressive forms express actions that start before another time or action and are in progress or incomplete.

PRESENT PERFECT PROGRESSIVE

| subject + has/have been
+ verb   + *-ing* |

The present perfect progressive is used for actions that started before the present and are still continuing now.

I *have been trying* to call you for over an hour. Who *have* you *been talking* to for so long?

PAST PERFECT PROGRESSIVE

| subject + had been
+ verb   + *-ing* |

The past perfect progressive is used for actions that started before and continued up to another past action.

Last month my neighbor quit her job. She said she *had been working* for the same company for seventeen years and was bored. In fact, she *had been thinking* about leaving for the last three years.

FUTURE PERFECT PROGRESSIVE

| subject + will have been
+ verb   + *-ing* |

The future perfect progressive is used for actions that will start before and continue up to another future action or time.

When I finish writing this book, I *will have been working* on it for five years.

Stative Verbs

Most verbs describe actions, which are temporary and changing, so they have a progressive form. However, some verbs describe conditions or states such as senses, feelings, ownership, mental processes, or measurements, which are considered permanent. These verbs, called *stative verbs,* are used only in the simple or perfect forms, never the progressive form. The following list shows some common stative verbs.

1. see, hear, feel, taste, smell (senses)
2. know, believe, understand, remember, appear, seem, prefer (mental processes)
3. want, love, hate, like, dislike, need, appreciate (emotions)
4. cost, equal, weigh, measure (measurements)

5. have, own, contain, belong, be (possession)

WRONG	*I am knowing that the book is costing five dollars.
RIGHT	I know that the book costs five dollars.
WRONG	*How much are you weighing?
RIGHT	How much do you weigh?
WRONG	*I'm hearing you, but I'm not understanding you.
RIGHT	I hear you, but I don't understand you.

However, some verbs can describe both an action and a state, such as *weigh, have,* and *see.*

STATE	I would like to come, but I *have* the flu.
ACTION	*I'm having* a party tomorrow. I hope you can come.

USING THE ENGLISH TENSE SYSTEM

English has three views of time: past, present, and future. Whenever we write, we choose one of these times as our base time. This base time then influences the tenses we choose as we write about what occurred before, during, or after the base time.

Once we establish a base time, we must keep it unless: we state a general truth (using the simple present) that temporarily suspends our base time; we use a time word or a phrase that clearly ends the old base time and replaces it with a new one; we change to another subject that requires us to shift time.

Base Time Is the Past

If our base time is the past, we say that anything that happens before this time occurs "in the past of the past" and that anything that happens after this time occurs "in the future of the past." The following table shows which tenses to use for the three possibilities.

BEFORE THE BASE TIME: PAST OF THE PAST	BASE TIME: PAST	AFTER THE BASE TIME: FUTURE OF THE PAST
past perfect past perfect progressive	simple past past progressive	English has no special verb forms to express this time. We use: simple past past progressive

Examples

The year before I *had started* the same course but never *finished* it. ← Last summer I *took* a Japanese course at the university. → After the course, we all *went* out for Japanese food.

| I *had started* to study six months earlier, so I *had been studying* a long time. ← | Last year at this time I *was taking* the TOEFL exam. → | Two weeks after the exam, I *was* still *thinking* about TOEFL questions. |

Analyzing Tenses

Look at the following passage. Double underline each verb and explain why the writer used that particular tense. Check your answers at the bottom of the page.

[1]When I turned 15, a very big change took place in my life; my father died. [2]I was alone and there was nobody to talk to. [3]I realized that I had lost one of the most important people in my life. [4]It was a very hard time for me. [5]Every day I wished that it hadn't happened, but I knew he was gone forever. [6]Eventually I learned to accept his death, but I still miss him now.

Base Time Is the Present

If our base time is the present, we say that anything that happens before this time occurs "in the past of the present" and that anything that happens after this time occurs "in the future of the present." The following table shows which tenses to use for the three possibilities.

BEFORE THE BASE TIME: PAST OF THE PRESENT	BASE TIME: PRESENT	AFTER THE BASE TIME: FUTURE OF THE PRESENT
present perfect present perfect progressive	simple present present progressive	simple future future progressive

Examples

| She *has lived* there since 1990. ← | Jessica *lives* in a very small apartment. → | She *is going to look* for a bigger place next month. |

| He *has been writing* letters and making phone calls. ← | Jonathan *is looking* for a job. → | Probably he *will* still *be looking* two months from now. |

Answers: 1. turned (base time: past), took (base time) died (base time) 2. was (base time), was (base time) 3. realized (base time), had lost (before the base time) 4. was (base time) 5. wished (base time), knew (base time), was (base time) 6. learned (after the base time) . . . had happened (before the base time), miss (present: general truth)

Analyzing Tenses

In the following passage, double underline each verb and explain why the writer used that tense. Check your answers at the bottom of the page.

¹Have you ever noticed how many words you say in one day? ²Have you ever measured how much time passes between closing your mouth and opening it? ³Many people speak from morning to night. ⁴They are afraid of silence. ⁵They think it means emptiness and that makes them feel helpless. ⁶But I think silence is beautiful. ⁷By letting my mouth rest, I can listen to the dancing of the wind and the singing of the water. ⁸I can listen to the small, clear sounds in my brain as I consider my problems. ⁹Silence is a free time in which I can create anything I want. ¹⁰In silence I am the master, the emperor. ¹¹Nobody can defeat me; I have the power to shape my dreams.

Base Time Is the Future

If our base time is the future, we say that anything that happens before this time occurs in the past of the future and that anything that happens after this time occurs in the future of the future. The following table shows which tenses to use for the three possibilities.

BEFORE THE BASE TIME: PAST OF THE FUTURE	BASE TIME: FUTURE	AFTER THE BASE TIME: FUTURE OF THE FUTURE
future perfect future perfect progressive	simple future future progressive	English has no special verb forms to express this time. We use: simple future future progressive

Examples

She *will have taken* more than 30 courses and *written* 50 essays. ← Lydia *will graduate* from college in 1999. → After graduation, she *will travel* for a year or two.

We *will have been traveling* for two weeks. ← Next month at this time we *will be flying* to Caracas. → We *will be staying* with friends, so we *will have* a car.

Answers: 1. have . . . noticed (before the base time), say (base time: present) 2. have . . . measured (before the base time); passes (base time) 3. speak (base time) 4. are (base time) 5. think (base time), means (base time), makes (base time) 6. think (base time), is (base time) 7. can listen (base time), is (base time) 8. can listen (base time), consider (base time) 9. is (base time), can create (base time), want (base time) 10. am (base time) 11. can defeat (base time), have (base time)

Analyzing Tenses

In the following passage, double underline each verb and explain the writer's choice of tense. Check your answers at the bottom of the page.

¹Yesterday I handed out the reading list for this course. ²Next week we will discuss the first article on the list. ³By then everyone should have finished reading it. ⁴You will also write a one-paragraph summary of the article which I will collect and grade. ⁵For the rest of the course, you will be responsible for one article each week so that by the end of the semester, you will have read, discussed, and summarized all the readings.

Practice Correcting Verb Errors

The passages below contain mistakes in verb tense and verb form. First, double underline all the verbs. Then, find the mistakes and correct them. Note: Not all the verbs are wrong.

Example

My best characteristic is that I am a very peaceful person. I am feeling most comfortable when I am playing with babies because they are the symbol of peace.

1. ¹My best quality is honesty. ²I always tell my friends the truth and I hope they believe what I say. ³I want them to trust me so I am thinking first I have to be honest. ⁴I am honest with my parents for the same reason. ⁵One time I want to go to my friend's house at night to do homework. ⁶I tell them my plan, but they say no because they worry when I go out at night. ⁷So my friend says she will drive me back home. ⁸Then my parents are agree to let me go. ⁹I think if I am honest, I can get what I want.

2.   [1]My last good quality is honesty. [2]I am honest with everybody. [3]For example when I worked last week, a lady leaved her purse in the store. [4]I put it in a safe place because I think maybe she come back. [5]I was right. [6]She come back one hour later. [7]I give it to her and she give me a $10 tip. [8]I think being honest is not only a way to get something, it is a good way to be.

3.   [1]One negative characteristic is that often I can't controlled myself. [2]For example, frequently I am deciding I will do exercises every morning, but then I am stopping after only three or four days. [3]Also, I am hurrying too much; I am driving too fast, eating too fast and working too fast. [4]Therefore I am making many mistakes.

4.   [1]Before I came here, I use to jog every morning with my father. [2]Whenever I jogged, I feeled fresh air and soft wind. [3]It made me feel really powerful. [4]But now I did not have any exercise for a few months. [5]Therefore I gained weight and I always feel tired. [6]Whenever I am thinking about my condition, I am deciding to exercise, but I can't. [7]The main reason is my laziness. [8]It is my worst quality.

EDITING PRACTICE

The following essay is the final draft that a student wrote for Project 1. The draft contains errors in basic sentence parts and verb tense and form. To find the errors, be patient and read the essay several times very carefully and critically, each time looking for a different kind of mistake. If you try to correct everything in one reading, you will miss many errors. Follow these steps to correct the errors.

1.   Read the whole essay to see what the writer is saying.
2.   Go back and mark the basic sentence parts: single underline the subject, double underline the verb, and put a wavy line under and/or brackets around the object or complement. The first sentence is completed for you. If you find any part that is missing or repeated, correct it.
3.   Look at each verb you double underlined. If you find a mistake in tense or form, correct it.

1   Some <u>people</u> <u>want</u> to be healthy. Some people would like to be wealthy. And

2   some people want to be wise. I think the best of these choices is wise.

3   Health it is good but is not very important because you could die at any

4   moment. You could die in an accident or killed by a robber. Death could come

5   when you don't expect it. My grandfather was having very good health, but one

6   day when he was only 56 years old, he was on a bus and the bus drived off the

7   road and he died.

8   Wealth it is very important. Everybody knows that money is the king of this

9   life. Whoever has money has everything they wanted. Whoever has money

10   could buy any physical thing they liked. But people who have money lose the

11   most important thing in this life: feelings. This is because the people who rich

12   always want more and more. They don't care about anyone else. Money is a

13   good thing to have, but love for other people is more important.

14   But a person who is wise he is a complete human. Is the nearest thing to

15   perfection. A wise person could be the poorest person in the world, he could be

16   sick, he could have no family, but his words are like gold. They are bringing

17   happiness and goodness. This is the kind of person I am wanting to be.

SUBJECT-VERB AGREEMENT

Basic Rules

The verb must agree with its subject whenever you use:

1. The verb *be* as a main verb in simple present or past tense or the verb
    have as a main verb in simple present tense.

    We *are* a family of teachers. My grandparents *were* teachers. My
    mother *was* a teacher. I *am* a teacher, and my sister *is* a teacher.
    I *have* two children; my sister *has* three.

2. Simple present tense of all verbs in third-person singular.

    Sandra loves chocolate cake.
    He lives in an apartment on Broadway and Eighth Street.
    That *woman* works in my office.
    The *air* smells very sweet today.

3. Compound tenses that include *be* or *have* as the first auxiliary.

    My *cat is sleeping* on my desk.
    My *dogs are sleeping* under the bed.
    Rain was dripping off the roof.
    Puddles were forming everywhere.
    Ron has been living here for twenty years.
    Joe and Ann have just moved here.

But note that:

1. When a modal auxiliary is used, there is no agreement. The main verb does not change form.

   He can *sing* very well, but *he* should *practice* more.
   She must *do* all the homework assignments.

2. When the subject and verb are reversed in order, the verb still agrees with its subject.

   In the park *were* two homeless *men* sleeping on the benches.
   Where *are* the *instructions* for the microwave oven?

3. The verb agrees with the simple subject regardless of any words that come between the simple subject and the verb.

   The *woman* across the street with the two dogs *is* my neighbor.
   One of the girls on the volleyball team *was* sick yesterday.
   Each of the students in the class *has to present* an oral report.

4. When *who, which,* or *that* is the subject, it takes a singular verb if the word it refers to is singular and a plural verb if the word it refers to is plural.

   Peter and Jane are two people *who love* to eat.

   Katherine is the kind of student *who* never *comes* late.

Special Cases of Subject-Verb Agreement

Unfortunately, languages are not always logical, and English has a number of cases where subject-verb agreement does not follow the rule that you might expect. The following table shows some of these special cases.

SUBJECT	SINGULAR VERB	PLURAL VERB	EXAMPLE
there	✔	✔	There *is* a telephone in every room. (singular noun) There *are* two beds in every room. (plural noun)
-one words one anyone everyone someone	✔		 One of the team members *is* sick. If anyone *wants* to help, call Jim. Everyone *is* invited. Someone *is knocking* on the door.
-body words nobody anybody everybody somebody	✔		 Nobody *has* time to help. If anybody *does* not *agree*, say so. Everybody *is going* to the football game. Somebody *has eaten* my candy.

20

SUBJECT	SINGULAR VERB	PLURAL VERB	EXAMPLE
-thing words nothing anything everything something	✔		Nothing *matters* in life but good health. Anything you can bring *is* helpful. Everything we owned *was* lost in the fire. Something *is going to happen* soon.
each	✔		Each of the chairs *has* a number. The books are expensive. Each *costs* $25.
either, neither	✔		I have an extra ticket if either of the girls *wants* to come. Neither of my cousins *has* ever *been* here.
plural words showing distance, money, or time	✔		Twenty *miles is* not a long distance by car. A million *dollars is* a lot of money. Three *hours* of English class *is* tiring.
arithmetical calculations	✔		Five plus five *is* ten. Two times five *equals* ten.
either . . . or	✔	✔	singular noun Either the *chairs* or the *table has to be moved*. plural noun Either the *table* or the *chairs have to be moved*
neither . . . nor	✔	✔	singular noun Neither my *parents* nor my *sister is coming*. plural noun Neither my *sister* nor my *parents are coming*.

SUBJECT	SINGULAR VERB	PLURAL VERB	EXAMPLE
not only . . . but also	✔	✔	Not only the *dogs* but also the *cat is* sick. [singular noun] Not only the *cat* but also the *dogs are* sick. [plural noun]
none of + plural count noun	✔	✔	None of the children *is* hungry. None of the children *are* hungry. None of my friends *wants* to see that movie. None of my friends *want* to see that movie.
all of + noncount noun	✔		All of the furniture *was loaded* on the truck. All of the snow *has melted*.
all of + plural count noun		✔	All of the houses *were built* at the same time. All of the trees *have started* to turn red.

some nouns ending in *-s*
   news
   series
   physics/ mathematics
   lens
	✔		The news *has* just *begun*.
			A series of mistakes *was made*.
			
			Physics *is* my favorite subject.
			The right lens of my sunglasses *is* scratched.

some nouns ending in *-s*
   pants
   jeans
 	
   scissors
 	
   glasses
		✔	Those pants *are* too long for her.
			His jeans always *have* holes in them.
			The scissors *have disappeared* again.
			My glasses *were* so dirty that I couldn't see.

Practice Correcting Errors in Subject-Verb Agreement

All of the following passages contain mistakes in subject-verb agreement. Single underline the subjects and double underline the verbs. Then correct any agreement errors that you find.

> **Example**
>
> *has*   *finishes*
> He <u>have</u> to <u>go</u> to work after <u>he</u> <u>finish</u> class.

1. Both speaking and writing are important for everyone who are interested in learning a language. If an ESL student knows how to write good English and don't have mistakes in grammar, but he can't communicates with other students because he don't speak English, then he will haves a lot of difficulty in his classes.

2. Nobody like to take tests. I don't either. However, I think it is a good idea that universities give students a writing test when they enter. Although that type of test have some disadvantages, I think everybody have to prove his ability to write before he start classes.

3. Reading and writing is very closely related. A person who read a lot is also a person who have a lot to write about. Reading expand your thoughts and give you new experiences. Also reading teach you that you are not the only person who suffer from problems in the world. You know there is many people who are in worse situations.

4. Reading is done in my head; nobody see it. But writing is done on the paper. Everybody look at it and everybody find the mistakes. So I am always embarrassed to write anything. Now I am taking this course. Two thousand dollars are a lot of money to spend to learn English, and twenty hours a week are a lot of time, but if I can learn to write better, neither the money nor the time are too much.

5. Writing is very important in our life. It makes communication easy and bring people closer to each other. Writing permit us to send messages to other people living far from us. It allow us to save ideas and thoughts for many years.

SENTENCE BOUNDARIES

Read the following passage.

> [1]One reason why writing is difficult for me is that there is nothing to help me express my ideas. [2]For example, in speaking if you want to ask someone the time. [3]You can just point at your wrist. [4]But in writing there is no body language, just words. [5]Which makes it more difficult.

Do you see any problems with any of the sentences in the passage?

1. Does every sentence begin with a capital letter and end with a period?
2. Does every sentence follow the rules about correct word order?
3. Is every sentence a clause? (Does it have at least one subject and verb?)
4. Is every sentence grammatically complete?

Now look at this passage and ask yourself the same questions:

> [1]Another problem is that I can't see the reader's reaction. [2]When he finishes reading. [3]I can't change his opinion. [4]I can't argue or convince him. [5]Because I am not present. [6]Somehow I feel he is judging my writing without giving me the opportunity to answer.

Independent and Dependent Clauses

In written English, *a sentence must always be a clause*. It must have at least one subject and one verb. However, there are two kinds of clauses.

An *independent clause* is a grammatically complete clause. It can be a complete sentence by itself, beginning with a capital letter and ending with a period.

> I first began writing poems in elementary school.
> My mother often read poems to me at night before bedtime.

A *dependent clause* is not grammatically complete. It can form part of a sentence, but it cannot stand alone as a whole sentence beginning with a capital and ending with a period. (Another name for a dependent clause is a *subordinate clause*.)

> when I first started writing
> because I loved the sound of the words

Answers: Passage 1. [2]For example, in speaking if you want to ask someone the time, [3]you can just point at your wrist. [4]But in writing there is no body language, just words, [5]which makes it more difficult. Passage 2. [2]When he finishes reading, [3]I can't change his opinion. [4]I can't argue or convince him [5]because I am not present.

Fragments

If you write a dependent clause as if it were grammatically complete (beginning with a capital letter and ending with a period), you are writing a sentence called a *fragment*. People often speak in fragments, but they are considered incorrect in formal writing.

> I started writing poems.
> *Because I loved the sound of the words.*

The first clause "I started writing poems" is an independent clause and can be a complete sentence. The second clause "Because I loved the sound of the words" is a dependent clause standing alone as a sentence. It is a fragment.

Note: The words listed below can begin dependent clauses. Whenever you start a clause with one of these words, be careful that you do not write a fragment. (Words that begin a dependent clause are called *subordinating conjunctions*.)

after	if	unless	whether
(al)though	in order that	until	which, whichever
because	since	what, whatever	while
before	that	when, whenever	who
how	so that	where, wherever	whose

How to Correct a Fragment

Usually you can correct fragment errors by attaching the fragment (dependent clause) to the sentence that comes before or after it, whichever makes better sense.

WRONG   *I find writing very difficult. After I have written two or three lines. I usually stop. Because I don't have anything to say about the topic.* Maybe brainstorming can help me find more ideas.

RIGHT   I find writing very difficult. After I have written two or three lines, I usually stop because I don't have anything to say about the topic. Maybe brainstorming can help me find more ideas.

WRONG   *I thought writing was just as easy as speaking. Until I came here and had to write essays.* Then I changed my mind.

RIGHT   I thought writing was just as easy as speaking until I came here and had to write essays. Then I changed my mind.

Punctuation Rule

When a dependent clause comes before an independent clause, put a comma after the dependent clause.

> dependent clause **,** + independent clause

When a dependent clause comes after an independent clause, no comma is necessary.

> independent clause + dependent clause

Practice Correcting Fragments

1. Go back to the passages on page 200. Find the fragments and see if you can correct them. Check your answers at the bottom of that page.

2. The passages that follow have problems with fragments. Read each passage carefully and decide which sentences are grammatically complete and which are fragments. When you find a fragment, underline it and correct it.

Example

Writing a letter in Chinese is not difficult for me. [,]

~~B~~ecause I don't have to worry about grammar and spelling.

1. ¹Once I took part in a writing contest. ²When I was a high school student. ³I had to write a composition about a certain topic within a limited time. ⁴When the contest began. ⁵I started to feel nervous. ⁶I felt a heavy stone was pressing on my mind. ⁷I had to squeeze my brain to decorate my composition with words that I didn't know well. ⁸And I had to read it over and over again. ⁹Because I would show it to others. ¹⁰Although I won a small prize. ¹¹It was really hard for me.

2. ¹At the beginning of the semester, I started to write a diary every night. ²But I couldn't continue. ³Because I used the same words so many times that I was bored. ⁴I know that if I want to be a better writer. ⁵I must learn a lot of new vocabulary. ⁶But often I am too lazy to do it.

3. ¹I have several close friends in my country. ²I sometimes call them to talk and they call me, too. ³But sometimes I feel I need to write them letters. ⁴Obviously, calling is more convenient than writing. ⁵Because it is so fast. ⁶However, writing letters is necessary. ⁷When I have some thoughts and feelings that can't be expressed well on the phone, or when I'm not in the mood to talk.

4. [1]I love to write diaries and letters and notes to myself because when I read them. [2]I can compare what I was to what I am, and I can evaluate myself. [3]My writing is my evidence.

5. [1]When I first started this course and I had to write essays in English. [2]I was really scared. [3]I had never done that before.

EDITING PRACTICE

The following essay is the final draft that a student wrote for Project 2. The writer has developed his ideas and organized them to his satisfaction. Now the grammar needs to be corrected. Remember that editing requires patience. You cannot do it all at once. Follow these steps to carefully edit the essay.

1. Read the whole essay so you understand what the writer is saying.
2. Go back and check the basic sentence parts: single underline the subject, double underline the verb, and put a wavy line under and/or brackets around the object or complement. Correct any errors you find.
3. Look carefully at all the verbs. Correct any errors in verb tense or form or in subject-verb agreement.
4. Look at each sentence to check for fragments.. Correct any that you find.

1   When I was in high school in my country. Teachers use to tell us that we have

2   to learn a special skill for writing. I did not understand what that special skill

3   could be. I thought that what you said you can write. But that is not true. When

4   I was ask to write in my native language. I realized that I cannot write well.

5   Writing and speaking, I realized, are very different skills.

6   I finished high school, but I still did not know much about writing. Then I

7   came to the United States. I thought that I know some English, so I won't have

8   any problems. Reading and speaking started well, but when I got to writing. I

9   experienced again the fact that I can't write. Writing was really hard. You can

10   even say that writing is a different language than speaking and you cannot

11   write exactly what you say.

12   There is many differences between writing and speaking. I think one impor-

13   tant difference is slang which we use in speaking and not in writing. On the

14   street, I heard people use the word "ain't" to make a sentence negative, but you

15   can never use such a word in writing.

16   Another difference is that when we speaking we can communicate our ideas
17   by intonation and body or facial movement, but in writing only different words
18   can do that. For example, when you want to show an emotion when are speak-
19   ing. You can do it by moving your hands or your head, but you have to use words
20   to show that in writing.

21   Moreover, the problem not over by knowing vocabulary. Those words must to
22   be well organized in sentences and those sentences have to be in the right place
23   in the paragraph and the paragraphs must to be in the right place in the whole
24   composition. Only then can you say that you have wrote something.

25   There is other differences between a composition and speaking Starting is
26   one of them. It is really hard in writing. You can start a conversation by saying
27   hello and keep going, but I think the introduction is the hardest part in writing.
28   Because it have to introduce what the essay all about and most important con-
29   vince the reader to read the rest of the essay.

30   Now I am understanding why I need a special skill to write. The reason is
31   that writing is different from speaking. It is also a skill play an important role
32   in our life. If you know how to write well and can make the reader believe in
33   what you wrote. If you know how to play with words. If you can write an impres-
34   sive letter to someone. It can changes your life.

Babak Nahavandi

MORE ABOUT SENTENCE BOUNDARIES

Read the following passage.

[1]From the newspapers that I read, I knew that America had a very powerful economy. [2] Also movies showed many rich people and also many middle class people who led comfortable lives. [3] Rarely I saw poor people, so I thought most of Americans have an opportunity to be successful. [4] Now I realize this country has serious social problems, rich and poor people have big differences between them. [5] A lot of homeless people live in the streets or subway stations, the wealthy people live in mansions with big gardens and a swimming pool. [6] It is a normal situation here. [7] My country is very poor, however, I seldom saw homeless people living in the street or train station. [8] During the

day I often could see beggars, but at night they usually had family or other place to sleep. [9] I ask myself who has the duty to solve this kind of problem in America — government or society?

Do you see any problems with any of the sentences in the passage?

1. Does every sentence begin with a capital and end with a period?
2. Does every sentence follow the rules about correct word order?
3. Is every sentence grammatically complete? (Does it contain at least one independent clause?)
4. In sentences with two or more independent clauses, are the clauses correctly joined?

Whenever you write a sentence with two or more independent clauses, you must join the clauses with an acceptable connecting word, acceptable punctuation, or both. But what English considers acceptable connecting words and punctuation may be very different from what they are in your native language.

Run-on Sentences and Comma Splices

If you write a sentence with two or more independent clauses but do not put an acceptable connecting word or punctuation between them, you have written a run-on sentence. If you write a sentence with two independent clauses and just put a comma between them, you have written a comma splice. Both are grammatically incorrect.

WRONG   *I hope to learn more about the good things here, I don't want to learn about the bad. [comma splice]

WRONG   *I came in the winter. When I got off the airplane, the temperature was minus 10° it was the coldest day of my life. [run-on sentence]

How to Correct Run-on Sentences and Comma Splices

There are three ways to correct a run-on sentence or a comma splice.

1. Divide the sentence into grammatically complete units and make each unit a separate sentence that begins with a capital letter and ends with a period.

                                            I

When I got off the airplane, the temperature was minus 10°. ~~it~~ was the coldest day of my life.

Answers: [4]Now I realize this country has serious social problems. Rich and poor people have big differences between them. [5]A lot of homeless people live in the streets or subway stations, and the wealthy people live in mansions with big gardens and a swimming pool. [7]My country is very poor. However, I seldom saw homeless people living in the street or train station.

2. If the ideas are closely related, put a semicolon (;) between the grammatically complete units.

>   When I first arrived, I felt very unsafe. I kept looking around me whenever I went outside. The environment was strange ; the faces and sounds around me were very unfamiliar.   ∧

>   Notice that the clause that follows the semicolon does not begin with a capital letter.

3. Put a comma plus an acceptable connector (*and, but, or, nor, so, for,* or *yet*) between the grammatically complete units. These connectors are called *coordinating conjunctions*. They are the only connectors that can follow a comma between independent clauses.

>   *but*
>   In my country, I was educated not to waste anything,∧now I waste plastic forks and knives, sugar and salt, and a lot of paper napkins.

Practice Correcting Run-on Sentences and Comma Splices

1. Turn back to the passage on pages 204–205. Find the run-on sentences and comma splices and correct them. Check your answers at the bottom of page 205.
2. All the passages that follow have problems with sentence boundaries. Read each passage carefully. Decide which sentences are correct and which have run-on sentences or comma splices. When you find a problem, correct it.

Example

>   *T*
>   I thought everyone was rich in this country. \the cities were
>   *and*
>   and full of cars and skyscrapers,∧everyone wore nice clothes.

1. [1]In my free time in China, I could watch tv, listen to the radio, or read books, however, in America, since I knew so little English when I first came and there were no Chinese programs on TV or radio and no Chinese books or newspapers where I was living, I spent all my free time just studying or staring out the window.

2. [1]When I told my best friend that I was thinking of staying in Ecuador, his words made me change my mind. [2]I will never forget what he said. [3]"Look at us, look at our clothes, look at our sad faces, in this country we just make enough money to buy necessities, we don't have the opportunity to buy nice things like you, we all wish we could go to the United States and you, stupidly, want to stay here. Here there is no future, we don't want you to become one of us."

3. [1]I didn't know what people were doing and thinking I didn't understand what they were laughing at and why. [2]I wondered if they were laughing at me. [3]I felt like a little animal who had suddenly landed in a strange forest full of traps.

4. [1]Here I often feel like a disabled person. [2]One time, I went to a fast-food restaurant and asked for a take-out meal of "potatoes with beef." [3]After I got the meal and walked out of the restaurant, I found the potatoes had no beef, so I went back and asked the restaurant to change my order. [4]But the clerk told me my English wasn't good, so he hadn't heard "with beef." [5]He said it was not his fault, so "no change." [6]I had never been insulted like that, I was so angry, I thought if my English had been good enough to argue with him and defend myself, maybe he wouldn't have discriminated against me.

AGREEMENT BETWEEN NOUN AND QUANTIFIER

In addition to agreement between the subject and verb, English requires agreement in number between a noun and any quantifying word or phrase that comes before it. The following list shows phrases in which a noun and its quantifier do not agree compared to phrases in which there is agreement.

Wrong	*Right*
*many book	many books
*several chair	several chairs
*a few apple	a few apples
*few friend	few friends
*three house	three houses
*a lot of sandwich	a lot of sandwiches
*one of the teacher	one of the teachers
*a group of student	a group of students
*a pair of shoe	a pair of shoes
*a row of chair	a row of chairs

Practice Correcting Errors in Agreement

The passages that follow contain mistakes in agreement between some of the nouns and their quantifiers. Read each passage carefully and circle every noun that has a quantifying word or phrase before it. If the noun and quantifier do not agree, correct the mistake.

1.   [1]During my first two semester at college, I made a number of good friend in my class. [2]But each time we started a new semester they spread among all the other classes, so we couldn't become really close friends. [3]This semester I decided to find new friends outside my class. [4]When I went to the cafeteria, I saw a group of Korean girl drinking coffee and talking. [5]It was easy to make friends with them. [6]So now I have Korean instead of American friends.

2.   [1]Since I was in junior high school in my country, Haiti, my dearest dream has been to go to a foreign country for my college education. [2]It is very difficult for a student to enter university in Haiti because there aren't enough college. [3]Only a very few student can get accepted. [4]Also the colleges in my country are not very good, so anyone who has studied in other country can get a better job.

3.   [1]In my mind, America was also a very dangerous place. [2]There were a lot of murder and bank robber and other problem such as drugs and AIDS here. [3]The crime rate was so high, I thought, that people could be killed at any time.

EDITING PRACTICE

The following essay is the final draft that a student wrote for Project 3. The writer has developed and organized her ideas well, but she has missed some grammar mistakes. Correct any errors you find, but do not change the writer's words or meaning. Remember that you must be patient to edit successfully. Follow these steps for careful editing.

1.   Read the whole essay to see what the writer is saying.
2.   Go back and mark the basic sentence parts: single underline the subject, double underline the verb, and put a wavy line under and/or brackets around the object or complement.
3.   Look at all the verbs and check verb tense, verb form, and agreement between subject and verb.
4.   Find all the nouns with preceding quantifiers and check agreement between the noun and its quantifier.
5.   Look at the sentences and check them for fragments, run-ons, and comma splices.

1   If anyone asks me what loneliness, nervousness, and homesickness means, I
2   can tell them. Since I came to the United States, I have experienced all these
3   feelings. They are feelings I will never forget.

4   I remembered on July 9, 1987 I got off the plane at Kennedy Airport. I was

5   standing there for twenty minutes not knowing what to do. I didn't even know

6   how to ask people where I should go next because of my poor English. All the

7   news I read about abduction, robbery, and other crimes in America came to my

8   mind. I felt really lost and scared, I suspected that something would happen to

9   me if I went the wrong way.

10   For the next few months I afraid of everything. I afraid to use the phone

11   because I couldn't understand what the operator said. I didn't even want to

12   take a bus. Because I didn't know where I should get off. I remember the first

13   time I tried to take a bus, I handed a dollar bill to the driver and I couldn't

14   understand why he wouldn't take. I didn't know that I had to have exact change

15   in coins. I thought something terrible would happen to me, so I just jumped off

16   the bus like a child who have done something wrong.

17   I didn't have friends for almost half a year. In the class, everyone talked, but

18   not me. I tried to speak English with my classmates, they wouldn't pay atten-

19   tion to me. I was really lonely. I had a lot of idea and thought which I wanted

20   to share with them, but I just couldn't communicate because of my language

21   problem. To tell you the truth, I probably spoke only two or three sentence in a

22   week. Every night I just sat in front of the TV. It made me more lonely some-

23   times. Because so many things on TV that I didn't understand and I didn't

24   know who I could ask or how to ask. Sometimes I thought I didn't belong in this

25   country.

26   I wrote many letters home. In every letter I said I would like to go back home.

27   I was missing my home so much that whenever I heard a plane passing over-

28   head, I wished I was in it flying home. Every day as I sat in class I thought

29   about what my parents and my friends doing at that moment. The more thought

30   about my home town, the more homesick I got.

31   Time has passed. Now day by day I get better at English. I try to overcome

32   those feelings that made me so unhappy at first. I know that I have to and I

33   believe I can. This country is not new for me now. Time is always a good helper.

Yu Hong

PRONOUNS

The following four paragraphs are from Tama Janowitz's essay that you read in Project 4. Circle all the pronouns (for example: *I, you, him, them, his, one, this, those*) and draw an arrow from each one to the noun or noun phrase it refers to (its *referent*). You should find 20 pronouns. Who is *I* in the first sentence?

1. In high school, I took a remedial English class—maybe it wasn't remedial, exactly, but without my knowing it, I had signed up for some kind of English class for juvenile delinquents.

2. But this class ended up being different; the main thing was that the teacher, Mr. Paul Steele, didn't seem to know he was teaching students who weren't supposed to be able to learn. He assigned the books—by Sherwood Anderson, by Hemingway, by Melville—and somehow by the due date everyone had read them and was willing to talk about them.

3. I remember another teacher, in graduate school, Francine du Plessix Gray, who taught a course called Religion and Literature—another subject in which I had no interest. But the way she spoke was so beautiful, in an accent slightly French-tinged. And because she was so interested in her topic, the students became interested, and her seminars were alive and full of argument.

4. Of course, I had many other fine teachers along the way, but the ones who stand out in my mind were those who were most enthusiastic about what they were teaching.

Why Do We Use Pronouns?

Pronouns are words that take the place of nouns (or noun phrases or clauses). Pronouns help to reduce repetition because the writer does not have to use the original word or words all the time. At the same time, they help to make writing more coherent by carrying an idea forward through a passage.

Errors in Pronoun Use

Three types of errors in pronoun use are common.

Error 1. Lack of Pronoun Agreement

A pronoun must agree in gender (masculine, feminine, or neuter) and number (singular or plural) with its referent.

I gave Mr. Lewis the book he asked for.

There is a pen on the floor. Whose is it?

These are the textbooks that you must buy for the course.

Practice Correcting Errors in Pronoun Agreement

The following sentences have errors in pronoun agreement. Circle the pronouns and draw an arrow to their referents. If a pronoun and its referent do not agree, correct the mistake.

Example

My school was very strict about uniforms. We could not even wear different color shoes. If we wore it, we were sent home immediately.

1. Because Iran is a conservative Islamic country, all the girls in my school had to cover herself from the top of her hair to the bottom of her legs.

2. In my high school class, I knew everyone and they knew me, but here I don't know anyone and they don't know me.

3. In college, a student can wear anything they want and take whatever course they want.

4. In my country, we had to take special exams to get into college. If we failed, we had to wait a whole year before we could take it again.

5. Almost everyone wants to go to college because afterward they can get a much better job and earn more money.

6. Nail polish, jewelry, and make-up were also not permitted. If we wore it, we were punished or even prevented from taking the final exam.

7. Everyone who had Mr. Chan as a teacher has their own terrible tale to tell. He was the worst teacher in the world.

Error 2. Unclear Pronoun Reference

A pronoun must also have one clear referent. If it has no specific referent, if it has several possible referents, or if the referent is too far away, readers will be confused.

> Since I speak Spanish as my native language, I wanted to take a Spanish literature class. But when I went to register, *they* told me that my English wasn't good enough.

Who are *they*? Advisors? Professors? The pronoun has no referent.

> All my life I have wanted to be a teacher. Every year since kindergarten, I have sat in a classroom and watched the teacher at work. None of the teachers knew it, but for the last twelve years, I have been their unpaid apprentice. I have learned everything from them. *It* is my dream in life and someday soon I will reach it.

What is *it*? The referent (to be a teacher) is so far away, we have forgotten it.

> My favorite year in school was third grade. Miss Ling, the best teacher in the school, was my classroom teacher, and Yan, my best friend, sat next to me. One day *she* asked me to help *her*.

Which *she*? Which *her*? Miss Ling or Yan? Both are logically possible.

Practice Correcting Unclear Pronoun Reference

In the following sentences, some of the pronouns do not have clear referents, causing confusion for the reader. Circle each pronoun and think about what it refers to. If you cannot find a clear referent, correct the problem.

1. [1]One difference between high school and college is that it gives students a choice of classes. [2]In high school, we had to take whatever classes they told us to take. [3]Every year for four years, we had to study math, history, science, language, and literature. [4]Even if we didn't like it or weren't very good at it, we still had to study it. [5]Here, however, we can choose whatever we are interested in studying.

2. [1]If teachers always get angry and impatient when students don't understand something and ask questions, they will never learn. [2]If they insult students in front of the whole class or ignore them and don't bother to answer, they will feel stupid.

3. [1]I have always been interested in history and I would like to continue studying it. [2]But I have decided to major in computer science because it doesn't offer many job opportunities.

Error 3. Shifting Point of View

All writers choose a point of view when they write. *Point of view* means the perspective from which a story is told or an idea is described or argued. There are three possible points of view: first person (*I* or *we*), second person (*you*), and third person (*he, she, it, they, one, anyone, someone*).

Look back at the essays on pages 77 and 135. What points of view do the writers use? What type of writing most often uses the first-person point of view? What kind of writing usually uses the third-person point of view?

To make your writing clear, you should not shift point of view unnecessarily. If you start writing in the first-person (*I*), do not change suddenly to second-person (*you*). If you start writing in the third-person (*he, she, it, they*), do not suddenly jump to second-person. Be consistent in your point of view.

The examples that follow illustrate shifting points of view and solutions.

Shifting Point of View	Consistent Point of View
I like to write because it helps *me* to express my feelings and reactions. When *I* see *my* feelings on paper, *I* can begin to understand them better. Also, writing is a way to communicate *your* thoughts to other people.	*I* like to write because it helps *me* to express my feelings and reactions. When *I* see *my* feelings on paper, *I* can begin to understand them better. Also, writing is a way to communicate *my* thoughts to other people.
All students have problems, but *those* who don't speak English well have special problems. Often *you* don't understand instructions and information that is told to *you* at meetings or over the telephone.	All students have problems, but *those* who don't speak English well have special problems. Often *they* don't understand instructions and information that is told to *them* at meetings or over the telephone.

or

All students have problems, but *those* of *us* who don't speak English well have special problems. Often *we* don't understand instructions and information that is told to *us* at meetings or over the telephone.

Look back at the essay you edited on pages 203–204. Do you see any shifts in point of view?

Practice Correcting Shifting Point of View

Here are some passages that cause problems for the reader because of shifting point of view. Circle the pronouns that show the writer's point of view. If the point of view shifts, correct the problem.

1. ¹One of my good characteristics is that I am always lively and bright. ²My friends all tell me that I always look happy. ³I like to hear that because I want to be looked at that way. ⁴These comments always make you feel good, and you can be kind to everyone because you are happy first.

2. ¹Also, I try to help other people when they are in trouble. ²I cannot just sit back and watch them; I have to go and help. ³I feel it is my responsibility to help other people when they need my help. ⁴Besides, they might help you in the future when you need their help.

3. ¹Usually we had all our classes in the morning. ²The afternoon was free time, but you couldn't leave the school. ³All the students had to study together in the same room.

4. ¹The best teacher I ever had was my high school chemistry teacher. ²She liked teaching; she liked her subject; she was very good at explaining things; and she was always friendly. ³You always had the feeling you could go and talk to her if you had a problem.

5. ¹My school was very strict. ²Students who came late or who did not do their homework had to stay after school and do extra work. ³No one could leave the room until you had finished all the extra assignments and the teacher had checked them.

6. ¹All the students in my country wore uniforms. ²At my school, you wore a blue wool jacket and skirt or pants and black shoes. ³You wore the same uniform all year, so in the summer we felt very hot.

PUNCTUATION

The following passage comes from a book about American culture, *American Ways* by Gary Althen. It is part of a chapter about teacher-student relationships at American colleges. Read the whole passage and think about your experiences. Have you had any of these problems?

1   "My [professor] wants me to call him by his first name," many
2   foreign . . . students in the U.S. have said. "I just can't do it! It doesn't
3   seem right. I have to show my respect."
4   On the other hand, professors have said of foreign students, "They
5   keep bowing and saying 'yes, sir, yes, sir.' I can hardly stand it! I wish
6   they'd stop being so polite and just say what they have on their minds."

7   Differing ideas about formality and respect frequently complicate rela-
8   tionships between American professors and students from abroad, espe-
9   cially Asian students. The professors generally prefer informal relation-
10 ships (sometimes, but not always, including use of first names rather than
11 of titles and family names) and minimal recognition of status differences.
12 Many foreign students are accustomed to more formal relationships and
13 sometimes have difficulty bringing themselves to speak to their teachers
14 at all, let alone call them by their given names.
15   The characteristics of student-teacher relationships on American cam-
16 puses vary somewhat, depending on the kinds of students involved—un-
17 dergraduate or graduate—and the size and nature of the school. Graduate
18 students usually have more intense relationships with their professors than
19 undergraduates do; at smaller schools student-teacher relationships are
20 usually less formal than they are at larger schools.

Look at the passage again and find all the different marks of punctuation. List
them below. (List each type only once.)

_____   _____

_____   _____

_____   _____

_____   _____

_____   _____

_____   _____

_____   _____

End Punctuation

The end of a sentence must be marked with a period (.), a question mark (?), or
an exclamation mark (!).

> American professors and foreign students have different ideas
> about formality and respect.

> Do you have any of these problems?

> I just can't do it!

Semicolon ;

The semicolon has two very different uses.

1. A semicolon can be used *between independent clauses* when the ideas are
closely related. The semicolon here is like a short period; it replaces a period,
never a comma.

> Graduate students usually have more intense relationships with
> their professors than undergraduates do; at smaller schools
> student-teacher relationships are usually less formal than they are
> at larger schools.

2.   A semicolon can be used *to separate items in a list* when the items are long or they already have commas in them. The semicolon here is like a long comma; it replaces a comma.

> For there does come along, on occasion, [a student] who is maybe at first a bit lost, certainly puzzled; who may well start out a Good Timer, an Egghead, a Performer, a Jock, a Medal Hound, a Gymnast, a Worker Ant; who may indeed have trouble settling on a major, who will be distressed by what sometimes passes for education, who might even be a temporary dropout; but who has a vital capacity for growth and is able to fall in love with learning, who acquires a taste for intellectual pleasure, who becomes in the finest sense of the word a Student.

Comma ,

A comma signals a short pause within a sentence. Although native English speakers do not always agree on where to use commas, there are five situations in which most English speakers use commas.

1.   A comma is used after introductory words, phrases, or clauses that come before the subject of the main clause of the sentence.

> Because many foreign students are accustomed to more formal relationships, they feel uncomfortable here.
>
> By the end of the semester, most students have adjusted.
>
> However, a few never do.

However, some writers omit the comma if the introductory phrase is short and expresses time or place.

> *At smaller schools* student-teacher relationships are usually less formal than they are at larger schools.

2.   A comma is used between independent clauses joined with a coordinating conjunction.*

	for	
	and	
independent clause,	**nor**	independent clause
	but	
	or	
	yet	
	so	

> My teacher asked us to call her by her name, *but* I couldn't.
>
> Other students were less formal than I was, *so* I copied them.

---

*Notice that the first letters of the coordinating conjunctions spell FANBOYS. Remembering this word can help you to remember the conjunctions.

However, some writers leave out the comma between short clauses joined by *and* and *or*.

> I called her Ms. Turkenik *and* my friends did too.

3. A comma is used between items in a list. The items can be words, phrases, or clauses.

> In my first year in university, I studied *mathematics, English, chemistry, and anthropology.*

> Mr. Cheng explained new information by *talking about it, writing it on the blackboard, and showing us pictures.*

Some writers put commas between all the items (as in the examples above); other writers leave out the comma between the last two items.

> I always *attended class, listened carefully and took notes.*

4. A comma is used to separate words, phrases, or clauses that are included as additional information in the sentence.

> Many foreign students . . . have difficulty bringing themselves to speak to their teachers at all, *let alone call them by their given names.*

> . . . the teacher, *Mr. Paul Steele,* didn't seem to know he was teaching students who weren't supposed to be able to learn.

Notice that when the additional information comes in the middle of the sentence, there must be commas before and after it.

5. A comma is used to separate quoted words from the rest of the sentence.

> "My [professor] wants me to call him by his first name," many foreign students . . . in the U.S. have said.

> On the other hand, professors have said of foreign students, "They keep bowing. . . ."

But never use a comma in these situations:

1. Never put a comma between a subject and a verb.

> WRONG   *The house that we live in, was built in 1864.
> RIGHT   The house that we live in was built in 1864.

2. Never put a comma between a verb and an object clause.

> WRONG   *The club members decided, that they would meet every Monday.
> RIGHT   The club members decided that they would meet every Monday.

3. Never put a comma after a coordinating conjunction.

> WRONG   *I offered to pay but, he insisted I was his guest.
> RIGHT   I offered to pay, but he insisted I was his guest.

WRONG *It was a cold, rainy day, so, I decided to stay home.
RIGHT   It was a cold, rainy day, so I decided to stay home.

Colon :

A colon is often used before a list or before an explanation.

> You have now tried three prewriting techniques to get your ideas down on paper: listing, free-writing, and asking wh– questions.

> But anyway, on the first day I figured out who this course was directed at: The students were surly and wore leather jackets, and the girls all had shag hair-dos. . . .

A colon can also be used before a quotation instead of a comma if the nonquoted words are an independent clause.

> . . . I heard myself saying this: "Not waste money that way."

Dash —

A dash is used to separate words, phrases, or clauses that are included as additional information in the sentence when

- the additional information itself has commas in it.
- the additional information is very different in structure.
- the writer wants to call attention to the information.

> There is the Performer—the music or theater major, the rock or folk singer—who spends all of his or her time working up an act. . . .

> I remember another teacher who taught a course called Religion and Literature—another subject in which I had no interest.

> It was one of the few times I had a teacher who spoke to me—and the rest of the class—with the honesty of one adult talking to others.

Be careful, however, not to overuse dashes; save them for special occasions.

Don't confuse a dash with a *hyphen*, a shorter line used to combine words (*student-teacher*) or to show a break between syllables when a word has been divided between two lines.

Quotation Marks " "

Quotation marks are used at the beginning and end of the exact words that someone said or wrote.

> They said, "Well, if you don't believe in God, then you're going to go to hell."

Quotation marks are also used to show that a word or phrase is being used with a special meaning.

> Once again I had signed up for something that looked easy, a "gut" course to fulfill the science requirement.

> . . . I have described [the kind of English my mother speaks] as "broken" or "fractured" English.

Notice that quotation marks always come in pairs, that they are always written at the top of the line, and that end punctuation generally comes inside the second quotation mark.

Special Note

Never separate a punctuation mark from the word that comes before it. If you cannot fit the punctuation mark at the end of the line, move the word before the punctuation mark plus the punctuation mark to the next line.

WRONG *I thought that failing the exam was the end of my life
. I was sure I would never be able to go to college.

RIGHT I thought that failing the exam was the end of my
life. I was sure I would never be able to go to college.

WRONG *Although I liked my high school teachers and classes
, I prefer college.

RIGHT Although I liked my high school teachers and
classes, I prefer college.

Practice with Commas

Here are the last two paragraphs from Amparo Ojeda's essay called "Growing Up American" from Project 3. Look at the commas the writer chose to use. Can you explain each of the commas in terms of the five comma rules summarized in the box?

Summary of Comma Rules

A comma is used:

1. After introductory information that comes before the main subject.

2. Between independent clauses joined with a coordinating conjunction.

3. Between items in a list.

4. To separate additional information in the sentence.

5. Between a quotation and the rest of the sentence.

---

1 American children, I observe, are allowed to call older people by their
2 first names. I recall two interesting incidents, amusing now but defi-
3 nitely bothersome then. The first incident took place in the university
4 cafeteria. To foster collegiality among the faculty and graduate stu-
5 dents, professors and students usually ate lunch together. During one
6 of these occasions, I heard a student greet a teacher, "Hey Bob! That
7 was a tough exam! You really gave us a hard time, buddy!" I was
8 stunned. I couldn't believe what I heard. All I could say to myself was,
9 "My God! How bold and disrespectful!"
10 Not long afterward, I found myself in a similar scenario. This time, I was
11 with some very young children of new acquaintances. They called to say
12 hello and to ask if I could spend the weekend with the family. At their
13 place, I met more people, young and not so young. Uninhibited, the chil-
14 dren took the liberty of introducing me to everybody. Each child who
15 played the role of "introducer" would address each person by his or her
16 first name. No titles such as "Mr.," "Mrs.," or "Miss" were used; we were
17 simply introduced as "Steve, this is Amparo" and "Amparo, this is Paula."
18 Because I was not acquainted with . . . American communicative style, this
19 took me quite by surprise. I was not prepared for the reality of being ad-
20 dressed as the children's equal. In my own experience, it took me some
21 time to muster courage before I could call my senior colleagues by their
22 first names.

The following paragraph is a continuation of the passage about teacher-
student relationships in American colleges. However, all the commas have
been removed. Add commas where they are necessary.

1 To say that student-teacher relationships are informal is not to
2 say that there are no recognized status differences between the two
3 groups. There are. But students may show their respect only in
4 subtle ways mainly in the vocabulary and tone of voice they use
5 when speaking to teachers. Much of their behavior around
6 teachers may seem to foreign students to be disrespectful.
7 American students will eat in class read newspapers and assume
8 quite informal postures. Teachers might not enjoy such behavior
9 but they tolerate it. Students after all are individuals who are
10 entitled to decide for themselves how they are going to act.

Practice with Punctuation

The next paragraph also comes from the passage about student-teacher relationships; it comes directly after the paragraph in the previous exercise. However, in this paragraph, all the punctuation has been removed. Decide where
the sentences begin and end, and add capital letters and end punctuation. Then
add any commas or other punctuation that is necessary.

1   American teachers generally expect students to ask them

2   questions or even challenge what they say teachers do not

3   generally assume they know all there is to know about a subject

4   nor do they assume that they invariably explain things clearly

5   students who want clarification or additional information are

6   expected to ask for it during the class just after class ends or in the

7   teacher's office at the times the teacher has announced as office

8   hours students who do not ask questions may be considered

9   uninterested or uncommitted

EDITING PRACTICE

The following essay is the final draft that a student wrote for Project 4. He has clarified and developed his ideas; now the essay needs editing. Follow these steps to carefully edit the essay. Correct any errors you find, but do not change the writer's words or meaning. Remember that with careful editing, you can find and correct many errors.

1. Read the whole essay to see what the writer is saying.
2. Go back and mark the basic sentence parts: single underline the subject, double underline the verb, and put a wavy line under and/or brackets around the object or complement.
3. Check every verb for verb tense, verb form, and agreement between subject and verb.
4. Find all the nouns with preceding quantifiers and check agreement between the noun and its quantifier.
5. Look at every sentence and check for fragments, run-ons, and comma splices.
6. Check all the pronouns for pronoun agreement, clarity of pronoun reference, and point of view.
7. Check punctuation.

1   Most American university students say they prefer college to

2   high school. They like to having more freedom to do what want

3   and they like to attending fewer classes and study what want. But

4   I am not agree with them. From my experience, I prefer high

5   school to college.

6   I attend high school in my country Colombia. In high school, I

7   was a friend of each student in my class. Everyone was a friend of

8   everyone else, all the students were growing up together, every

9   student knew the name of every other student, everyone was going

10   to break and to lunch together. I was on the soccer team and when

11   we went to other schools play against other teams. Many students

12   came to watch and cheer for us. We went to parties together and

13   sometimes we met in one person's house to do the homework

14   together. This were unforgettable years. I still remember the

15   name of each student in the school and I can still see their face in

16   my mind.

17   When I came to the United States everything was changing in

18   my life. My life and experience here at Queens College is very

19   different from high school. Outside my ESL class nobody know

20   anybody, I don't know the names of the others students and they

21   don't know my name. I don't know about any activities in this

22   college and nobody help me, I'm trying to get on the college soccer

23   team but when I go to register they tell me the office is closed.

24   Even the other student from my country are not friendly. I want to

25   join the Spanish Club but nobody can giving me information about

26   them.

27   I think when an American say they prefer college to high school

28   is because they finished high school in the same country that are

29   studying college in. If I stay in Colombia I think I will feel the

30   same. But in my case I came from another country with a different

31   culture and different language. College is very difficult for me and

32   so I prefer my high school experiences.

Teo Torres

Acknowledgments (*continued from the copyright page.*)

"Simplicity" by William Zinsser from *On Writinq Well,* 4th ed. Copyright 1976, 1980, 1985, 1988, 1990 by William Zinsser. Reprinted by permission of the author.

Excerpt from "Talking About Writing" copyright © 1976, 1979 by Ursula K. Le Guin; excerpted from "Talking About Writing," a speech delivered in Reading, England and Southern Oregon College; reprinted by permission of the author and the author's agent, Virginia Kidd.

The Maker's Eye: Revising Your Own Manuscripts" by Donald M. Murray. Reprinted by permission of the author.

"How to Write a Personal Letter." Reprinted by permission of International Paper.

"Test for a Genuine Writer" by Pamela Margoshes. Reprinted by permission of the author.

"Growing Up American: Doing the Right Thing" by Amparo B. Ojeda. Permission to reprint by Amparo B. Ojeda, Ph.D. The article first appeared in Wadsworth Anthropology Series *Distant Mirrors: America as a Foreiqn Culture.*

Adaptation of "Culture Shock and Alienation Remain Problems for Many Foreign Students on U.S. Campuses" from *The Chronicle of Hiqher Education.* Copyright 1990, *The Chronicle of Hiqher Education.* Reprinted with permission.

"Public School No. 18: Paterson, New Jersey" from *Winter Light* by Maria Gillan. Reprinted by permission of the author and Chantry Press.

Excerpt from "Silent Dancing," by Judith Ortiz Cofer is reprinted with permission from the publisher of *Silent Dancing: A Partial Remembrance of a Puerto Rican Childhood* (Houston: Arte Publico Press - University of Houston, 1990).

"Like a Rolling Stone" by Bob Dylan. Copyright © 1965 by Warner Brothers Music. Copyright renewed 1993 by Special Rider Music. All rights reserved. International copyright secured. Reprinted by permission.

Excerpt from *The Joy Luck Club* by Amy Tan. Copyright © 1989 by Putnam Publishing Group. Reprinted by permission.

"He Rocked, I Reeled" by Tama Janowitz. Reprinted by permission of International Creative Management, Inc. Copyright 1989 by Tama Janowitz.

Excerpt from "How Do We Find the Student . . ." by James T. Baker. Originally published in the *Chronicle of Hiqher Education.* Reprinted by permission of the author.

"Undecided — and Proud of it," by Michael Finkel. Originally published November 23, 1989 Op-Ed. Copyright © 1989 by The New York Times Company. Reprinted by permission.

Excerpt from "Workers of the World, Relax" by Bob Black. Originally published by Semiotext(e).

Excerpt from "Money and Freedom," by Marshall Glickman. Originally published April 26, 1987, *The New York Times Magazine.* Copyright © 1987 by The New York Times Company. Reprinted by permission.

"Student-Teacher Relationships" from Gary L. Althen, *American Ways,* (1988) Yarmouth, ME: Intercultural Press. Used with permission.

INDEX